FLANNEL-GRAPH JESUS

MORE THAN A ONE-DIMENSIONAL SAVIOR

PHIL AYRES

Printed in the United States of America

First Printing: January, 2018

ISBN 978-0-9998577-0-0

The Bible Revealed Publishing
150 Sunset Dr
Longwood, FL 32750

philayres.me

Cover Design: JimLePage.com
Publishing and Design Services: MartinPublishingServices.com

For my wife, Stefanie.
You make everything good in my life possible.

ACKNOWLEDGEMENTS

This work would not have been possible without these amazing people:

JEFF GOINS AND THE TRIBEWRITERS GROUP: I'm so glad I took the leap and joined TW. I found the encouragement I needed and the support to overcome my self-doubt.

TO MY AMAZING BETA-READERS: Shannon Veurink, Lucie Winborne, Jesse Barnett, and Pastor Eric Scholten. Thank you for reading my manuscript first and providing clear and helpful feedback.

TO MY KICKSTARTER BACKERS: Wow, you blew me away with your faith and generosity. Special thanks to Pastor Jan Puterbaugh, Mark Mathis, Chip Ware, Brian & Kathy Stout, Chuck & Jo Ayres, Mike & Rachel Johnston, David Lundberg, Maxine Wegner, Mark & Carole Caraker, and Michael Musselman.

TO MY PUBLISHING TEAM: Thanks to Melinda Martin for encouragement and beautiful interior design; Stacey Covell for careful and professional editing; Twila Bennett for indispensable advice and support; Shayla Raquel for counsel and guidance; Deanne Welsh for a push in the right direction; Dylan Kraayanbrink for advice on recording; and Joseph Thompson for his friendship, encouragement, and for writing the foreword.

AND LASTLY, TO MY AMAZING CHURCH FAMILY:
It's been thrilling to witness your focused attention on Jesus and your resulting faithfulness in our community. Thanks for your love and support over the years. Keep on being a great church.

CONTENTS

FOREWORD

BACK IN 2012 OR SO my friend Phil Ayres and I began a podcast we named *Former Pharisees*. Having both been pastors at thriving mega churches, and now both leading... let's just say, smaller congregations, we'd begun to ask ourselves the tough questions about ministry such as, would we keep doing what we were doing even if our churches never blossomed to thousands of attendees? As we examined some of our previously held beliefs, we realized that we were "recovering" Pharisees and had unwittingly become part of the "machinery" of Christianity ourselves, abandoning the true heart and essence of the message of Christ.

Our podcast led us to explore what it meant to be faithful to a calling no matter how difficult the season, and our exploration led us to many deep conversations about faith, relationships, and Jesus. For one, we agreed that some Christians had become so judgmental we were finding it hard to gain traction and credibility amongst people who didn't share our faith.

Two years later, Phil asked me if I'd be willing to teach one of the messages in a new series he'd started at his church titled, "Don't Know Much About Jesus." He asked me to teach on the topic, "Didn't Know Jesus Was A Rebel." I don't know if it's because my life spoke volumes to Phil about being rebellious, but hey, since I got to ride my Harley

Davidson Heritage Softail Classic down the center aisle of the auditorium onto the stage, I was hooked.

So when Phil asked me to write the foreword for a book covering the series we'd preached, I agreed without hesitation. So why this book, I hear you ask? With the myriad books out there about Jesus, why on earth should you read this one? I'm glad you asked because I'm dying to tell you.

According to the Pew Research Center, fully one-in-four members of the millennial generation—so called because they were born after 1980 and began to come of age around the year 2000—are unaffiliated with any particular faith. Indeed, millennials are significantly more unaffiliated than members of Generation X were at a comparable point in their life cycle (20% in the late 1990s) and twice as unaffiliated as baby boomers were as young adults (13% in the late 1970s).[1]

Clearly this indicates a crisis of faith about which many have written copiously. So how do we arrest this trajectory away from faith? Phil's book helps us answer that question. You see, Phil shows us that the way many Christians have portrayed Jesus to our world makes Him not only unattractive, but weak, ineffectual, and too serious. In reality though, Jesus was funny, friendly, though not always conforming, heck, He was a captivating communicator who cared deeply about other people's struggles. Rather than a

---

1   Allison Pond, Gregory Smith, Scott Clement, "Religion Among the Millenials," *Pew Research Center,* http://www.pewforum.org/2010/02/17/religion-among-the-millennials/ (accessed Dec 10, 2017).

Christianity that was exclusive and available only to a few, Jesus's approach to ministry was inclusive. This is one of the things I love about this book. Flannel-Graph Jesus doesn't skirt around the issues of faith, but makes it abundantly clear everyone is welcome to belong before they believe.

Phil answers our questions by taking us on an engaging journey through stories in the Bible as well as personal stories, helping us connect the dots with so many of the ignored attributes of Jesus that made Him so attractive to people who didn't even know Him. Then, with witty candor and characteristic probity he reminds us that, as Christ followers, we are called to look just like Jesus.

But what is it that makes Phil the right voice to be speaking about bridging the chasm between the Church and the non-believer? Having faithfully served as lead pastor at LifePoint Church for 11 years, and having raised two millennial children who love Jesus and are living committed lives as Christ followers, there's no doubt that Phil knows exactly what it looks like to bridge the gap between the message of the Gospel and the world, across generations.

So if your goal is to deepen your intimacy with Jesus so that you're better equipped to understand how to navigate life as a "Former Pharisee," or if your goal is to become more aware of how to connect with others who are outside of your faith experience, or even if your goal is simply to better understand who Jesus was, and is, and how His life can place you on a more fulfilling life trajectory, then this book is the perfect place to start your journey of discovery.

I invite you to take the journey away from being a Pharisee and join the growing fold of Former Pharisees who are discovering Jesus afresh! Happy discovering.

Joseph Thompson,
January 2018
Executive Director of Spiritual Development,
Action Church, Winter Springs, FL
Author, *I'm A Christian, So How Can I Have Demons?*

INTRODUCTION

THERE'S NO SHORTAGE OF TOPICS when it comes to preaching. Still, having served as a pastor in a small church for about 15 years, finding new material is sometimes a challenge. This is exactly the situation I found myself in at the end of 2013. I was just about to finish a 6-week series in Habakkuk and was trying to figure out what to preach about next.

The following Sunday I was approached by a young woman in the congregation who wanted to know where to start reading in her Bible. What a great question! First of all, the idea that someone *wants* to read their Bible thrills me. She wanted to know more but she wasn't sure where to start.

I asked her a few questions to learn what she might already know about faith and the church. Her answer was simple but profound. She said, "I've been in church for a long time, but I don't know much about Jesus."

I loved her honesty. I doubt most Christians would be so candid. Right away I knew I would develop a teaching series based on her statement. I wanted to help her and the rest of the congregation see Jesus for the man and Savior he is. But here's what shocked me, along the way I realized I had some things to learn about Jesus too.

I have always known about Jesus. I made a profession of faith and was baptized when I was 12. However, the Jesus I had learned about during my Sunday school years was relatively simple. I suppose it's nobody's fault. I'm sure my Sunday school teacher did her best to teach us kids every week. She taught us that Jesus loved us, and he loved other people too. She taught us Jesus was kind and gentle, and, from the pictures in our books, he was very clean.

Over the years my faith grew, but my understanding of Jesus stayed pretty much the same. It was as if my understanding of him stayed locked safely in a church storybook. Jesus remained calm. He stayed nice. He was tame and very serious too. After all, he saved us from our sins and there's nothing funny about that.

I called my teaching series, "Don't Know Much About Jesus" (quoted from the woman I talked to earlier). Every week I dug into the Bible to study Jesus like never before. Then I would teach the congregation whatever unknown or inspiring characteristics I could find. The result? Jesus is far more interesting than you might think or remember.

But, this new Jesus caught me off-guard. At times, I wasn't sure how I felt about this Jesus. He was abrasive with certain people. He was also very blunt. He was definitely not politically correct. Plus, he was tougher than I had pictured him, and rebellious too. In the end I came to really appreciate this new Jesus. I had always loved him, but now I was starting to like him too.

Maybe it's the same for you? Maybe you've been in church for a long time and have been a follower of Jesus almost as long. Perhaps you gave your life to Christ after realizing he loved you enough to die for your sins. Surely anyone who loved you that much deserved to be loved back. But, does the Jesus you picture deserve more than just devotion?

To answer the question; yes, it's possible, even probable. After we spend time combing through the many Gospel narratives telling us about what Jesus did and said; I think you'll find him irresistible. I'm confident by the time you finish the book you'll not only have a Savior; you will have a good friend too.

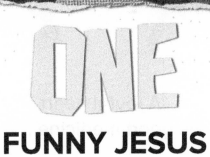

FUNNY JESUS

MORE THAN A ONE-DIMENSIONAL SAVIOR

"A joyful heart
is good medicine..."

—Proverbs 17:22a

"Laughter is the
best medicine.
But if you're laughing
for no reason,
you need medicine."

—Not Will Ferrell
(@itswillyferrell)

RECENTLY, I WAS FINISHING A round of golf with a couple friends when one of them began telling us a joke.

He said, "Jesus, Moses, and an old man were playing a round of golf when they came to the first hole. Jesus hit a perfect shot right down the middle of the fairway. Moses hit his shot straight towards a pond, which parted so the ball could roll right through and into the short grass. The old man stepped up to the tee and hit his shot way to the left.

Suddenly though, the ball bounced off a tree and was picked up by a squirrel. The squirrel was grabbed by a hawk, which lifted the squirrel and the ball into the air and flew over the green. The squirrel dropped the ball, which bounced twice, and rolled right into the cup. Moses rolled his eyes and told Jesus, 'You know, I really hate playing golf with your Dad.'"

Upon hearing this joke you probably fall into one of two groups: You might have laughed, or at least chuckled; or, you might feel it's sacrilegious to mention Jesus or God in a joke. If you fall into the latter category I encourage you to lighten up a little. It's okay to have a sense of humor; after all, your sense of humor is God-given. You are made in God's image, so if you have a sense of humor it's only because God has one too. This is a trait he passed on to all of his children, including Jesus.

I'll bet you didn't know Jesus was funny. It almost sounds wrong to say it, but it is true. Jesus was a really funny guy. I don't mean he was funny like a clown or a comedian. What I mean is he had a great sense of humor and he wasn't afraid to use it. It's one of the reasons so many people liked him.

That's right. People actually liked Jesus. True, there were a few people who didn't (we'll talk about them later), but many people, if not most people, thought he was a great guy.

Jesus was affable. That means he was approachable and cool. He was gracious and good-natured. I can see the look on your face now. You're thinking, really? That's not how I picture Jesus. That's because it's likely someone, somewhere, helped you fashion an inadequate picture of Jesus in your mind. My goal in this book is to help you erase this false image and replace it with a more accurate picture of Jesus. A biblical one.

My first ideas about Jesus were created through the flannel-graph. Most people nowadays don't even know what that is, but if you were raised in the evangelical church between 1950-1985 then you might be smiling right now. The flannel-graph was a board covered with—you guessed it—flannel. The Sunday school teacher would stick paper Bible characters onto the flannel and teach the Bible lessons. It was an early church version of multimedia.

The flannel-graph version of Jesus always looked pretty stoic. Flannel-graph Jesus always wore a beaming white robe with a blue sash. His hair was brown and long—longer than anyone I knew—and he was so serious. Maybe it was the way the Sunday School teacher communicated, I'm not sure. Whatever it was, I was always a little terrified of flannel-graph Jesus.

You might have a similar picture of Jesus in your mind, but perhaps it comes from a different source. TV versions of

Jesus haven't helped create an accurate picture of him either. The popular 70's film, *Jesus of Nazareth*, had us all believing Jesus was British. I don't know what it is about that posh accent but the actor playing Jesus in the film seemed pretty aloof. He spoke with the urgency of a man in need of tea and crumpets. Plus, I don't think he ever smiled.

Another area we can receive bad information about Jesus is from preaching. I'm guilty of this myself—I'll admit it. Sometimes preachers portray Jesus as some kind of superhuman character—so darn good he's no fun to be around. Don't get me wrong, Jesus is incredible and all-powerful. But don't make the mistake and picture him like a caped crusader on some mission from another planet. Jesus was fully human while being fully God. Because he was fully human, Jesus had

> IF HE HAD THE FULL RANGE OF HUMAN FEELINGS AND EMOTIONS, THEN HE MUST HAVE LAUGHED TOO. YES, JESUS HAD A SENSE OF HUMOR.

all the emotions we have. He felt joy, sadness, excitement, and anger. His humanity also means he felt pain, fatigue, hunger, and thirst. If he had the full range of human feelings and emotions, then he must have laughed too. Yes, Jesus had a sense of humor.

LIFE OF THE PARTY

Right in the middle of my second year of Bible college, a new kid transferred to our school. His name was Carl. Carl wasn't exactly like the rest of us. We were Bible-school geeks, but Carl was cool. He had just gotten saved, but before that, he had been a serious party animal.

A lot of students at the Bible college didn't know how to take Carl. Yes, he was a passionate Christian, but he was so new at it he was still rough around the edges. He wore shirts with inappropriate messages on them. He couldn't find any of the books of the Bible, and when he got mad he cussed. While many of the Bible college students didn't get along with him very well can you guess who did? Just about everyone else. There was something about Carl that set people at ease. Looking back, I think it was because he was so real and unpretentious. Exactly the opposite of us stuffy Bible college folks.

Here's something to ponder: Who was it that liked Jesus the most? Who wanted to be around him more than anyone else? That should tell us a lot about his personality. For example, there were two groups Jesus is often associated with in the scriptures. The first group is children. Kids loved Jesus. There is a story in the Bible where parents were bringing their kids to see Jesus (Matt. 19:13-15). I picture it the way parents bring their kids to see Santa Claus around Christmas. Imagine a line of children, all of them smiling and curious to get a moment with Jesus. In the story, his disciples were shooing the kids and parents away. But Jesus said, "Let the little children come to me and do not hinder them, for to such belongs the kingdom of heaven" (v. 14). Over and over in the gospels Jesus tells his followers the best way to understand faith is to be like a child. And, what do children like to do? Laugh. Run. Play.

Children must have liked Jesus because he was fun to be around, and he made them feel good about themselves. Now, think back to when you were a kid and see if you can remember your favorite teacher in elementary school. Why did you like him or her? Because they were so serious all the time? No. You liked them because they made you feel special and probably because they also had a sense of humor.

Children also felt safe being with Jesus. He was protective of them. One time he told his followers whoever would humble himself and become like a little child would be the "greatest in the kingdom of heaven" (Matt. 18:4). But, whoever leads a child astray, Jesus says it would be better off if they were already dead (Matt. 18:6). Jesus was very serious about protecting the innocence of children.

The other group of people who liked to be around Jesus were sinners. This doesn't sit well with some people today and frankly, it didn't sit well with people in Jesus's time either. But Jesus didn't come to win a popularity contest. He came to save people, and if that meant he had to mingle with some people of bad reputation—so be it. Jesus loved to be with them and they loved to be with him.

In Luke 19:1-10, Luke tells about a man named Zacchaeus. Zacchaeus was a well-known thief and turncoat. When he heard Jesus was passing by he was so interested in seeing him he climbed into a nearby tree so he could get a good look at the Savior. When Jesus passed below he noticed Zacchaeus in the tree and said to him, "Zacchaeus, hurry and come down, for I must stay at your house today" (v. 5). Right away Zacchaeus came down and Jesus was a guest in his house. Actions like these earned Jesus the nickname "friend of sinners" (Luke 7:34).

The point I'm making here is that sinners don't usually want to spend time with a person who is boring, serious, and judgmental. Actually, nobody wants to spend time with a person like that. The people Jesus befriended were considered sinners because of their bad reputation. They gained their bad reputations through their actions and choices. Some were prostitutes. Some were thieves. Some had loose morals. They lived outside of the moral code.

Remember, though, Jesus didn't join them in their sinful practices. He befriended them and offered them something better than their sin. He offered forgiveness and redemption if they would accept him.

PICK UP THE PHONE

We all have that one friend—you know the one I'm talking about. He or she is the one who calls, and we just look at our phones and say, "Not now, I just don't have time for this." Maybe it's because they always bring up some issue they have with the friendship, or maybe they need something you just can't give them. Whatever it is, you find the friendship to be a lot of work and the effort is usually one-sided. In moments like this, we might send the call to voicemail or respond with a simple text.

What if Jesus called you on the phone today? How excited would you be to take the call? Would you be worried he would have a rebuke for you? Would you be worried he would want to discuss some sin issue you have been dealing with lately? Would you be worried that somehow, he would be disappointed with you? If you feel like you might be tempted to send Jesus to voicemail you may have an inaccurate picture of Jesus in your mind.

In the gospels, people were always excited to talk to Jesus. They followed him and called out to him. They were desperate to touch him. With the exception of the Pharisees, everyone was glad to talk with him. No one felt judged, regardless of their past. Jesus himself said, "For God did not send his Son into the world to condemn the world, but in order that the world might be saved through him" (John 3:17).

Knowing that Jesus did not come to condemn us is important. It's important because it can change our view of him from a sullen and serious savior to a humorous and loving friend. Jesus wants to be the kind of friend you open up to. He wants to be the kind of friend that gives as much, more even, to the relationship as you do.

A MIGHTY WIND

As I mentioned earlier, this book is the result of a teaching series I preached several years ago. In the middle of one of my messages I was making the point that Jesus was human, therefore he had regular bodily functions. Then I did something that caused quite a stir in the congregation. I said, "Jesus farted." Many people laughed loudly, but some were very offended. A few even stopped attending the church!

Maybe you are offended too. However, before you put this book down or burn it as heresy please hear me out. Part of understanding the real Jesus is knowing and coming to grips with the fact that he was fully human, and that human beings fart. They toot. They pass gas. However you want to say it, it's true. And, by the way, farts are funny. They are funny to kids, teens, men, and even some women too!

During his ministry on Earth, Jesus traveled with twelve disciples. These disciples were men and they walked everywhere they went. Plus, they camped outside and often cooked by fire. It is impossible for me to believe that over the course of almost 1,000 days and nights together, these ragtag bunch of men, many of whom were fishermen, didn't get a laugh or two by breaking wind around the campfire.

You might be saying, "No way! My Savior would never do such a thing." Well, keep reading. What's at stake here is actually a much larger issue that crept up in the 3rd century. It's called Docetism. Docetism is the belief that Jesus was never fully human. Instead, Jesus was some kind of spirit who only appeared to be human. Third century docetists believed Jesus was more like an apparition or a ghost.

The genesis of this belief began with the notion that the body is inferior to the spirit. Because people couldn't imagine Jesus having normal bodily functions, they assumed he wasn't fully human. This is a problem, because if Jesus was only a spirit, he couldn't have died. If Jesus didn't die, then he couldn't be raised from the dead. And, if he wasn't raised from the dead this means we are still dead in our sins today (1 Cor. 15:17). See the problem?

Part of knowing the real Jesus is understanding he wasn't some kind of untouchable and unapproachable superhuman, spirit being. Even though he was the son of God, he was fully human in every way. Get that? Every single way. Remember that next time you pass gas!

ANCIENT WIT

So maybe you're saying, "Okay, I get it—Jesus was approachable. But I can't think of a time when he said anything funny." That's understandable. However, remember that when we read the Bible we do so from our own Western cultural viewpoints. Many Hebrew ideas are lost on us. Most people also don't know much about Greek, which is the original language of the New Testament. Sometimes it's important to dig a little deeper into some of the words and stories of Jesus to find comedy gold, so to speak.

Mark provides one such interesting example in chapter seven of his gospel. He records a conversation Jesus had with some Pharisees and Scribes. These religious leaders were after Jesus. They were always trying to trip him up.

Jesus and his disciples had been traveling and had just arrived from Jerusalem. Someone had provided some food for them and the disciples, all grungy and dirty, started to eat. However, they didn't wash their hands first.

It's important to note that in the 1st century there were many ceremonial rules for the Jews. There was a rule for just about everything. This included eating. Every good, religious Jew was required to wash their hands in a certain way before eating. If one really wanted to take it to the next level, there was even a special washing ritual for the cups, bowls, and plates. This ceremonial washing rule was not a part of God's original law, but a later addition of rules created by the rabbis over the years and was followed by Hebrew men and women for centuries.

The Pharisees confronted Jesus on this point saying, "Why do your disciples not walk according to the tradition of the elders, but eat with defiled hands?" (Mark 7:5).

Jesus responded to them by quoting the Bible (v. 6-13). His statement is nothing short of an epic burn. He quoted the prophet Isaiah, who lived almost seven centuries earlier and prophesied about people who would teach "as doctrines, the commandments of men" (v. 9, cited from Isa. 29:13). His point was that ceremonial hand washing was not something God required of people, but a man-made rule.

Jesus went on to explain about purity and cleanliness. He said, "Do you not see that whatever goes into a person from outside cannot defile him, since it enters not his heart but his stomach, and is expelled?" (Mark 7:19). To you and me that sounds pretty tame. However, when you look at the original language it's more graphic. Jesus was speaking Aramaic when he said this and the account was later written down in Greek.

The Greek word used here for expelled is, *aphedron*. Aphedron is a compound word that is made up of two other words: *apo*, which means expel, and *hedraois*, which means to sit. You guessed it, the easiest and closest translation we have for this word is "toilet" or "latrine."

But Jesus is talking about more than bodily functions, he's referring to words—the things we say. This is because the things we say are born out of our thoughts and emotions. If evil thoughts and selfish emotions drive your words, then what you expel defiles you. Jesus was comparing the unwarranted religiosity of the Pharisees to excrement. So, what was Jesus really saying to the Pharisees? Simply put, they were full of...well, you know.

Right after this happened, Mark records another interesting interaction Jesus had, this time with a woman. This passage is often misunderstood, especially if you don't realize that Jesus had a sense of comic timing. Without considering Jesus's sense of humor he comes off like a jerk. In chapter 7:24-30, Jesus traveled to Tyre. This is a coastal town north of Jerusalem. Most of the people he would meet at this location were not Jews, but Gentiles.[2]

When Jesus arrives, he tries to hide away in a house, perhaps to get some rest. But a local woman finds out about his arrival and comes to him for help. Mark says, "she fell at his feet" and "begged Jesus to drive the demon out of her daughter" (Mark 7:25-26).

Jesus says, "Let the children be fed first, for it is not right to take the children's bread and throw it to the dogs" (v. 27).

Did he just call her a dog? Yes, I think he did. It sounds even worse when you understand dogs weren't the lovable, cuddly, and playful pets we see them as today. They were mostly strays, populating the cities and towns. They were filthy, hungry, and detested.

So why does Jesus respond this way? Most interpretations involve the idea that the children represent Israel, the food represents Jesus, and the dogs are the Gentiles. At some level, this is true. This makes perfect sense because Jesus has described himself as food (John 6:35) in the past and the Gentiles were typically reviled by the Jews. This interpretation though, makes Jesus's response to her particularly harsh.

However, some take this account literally, meaning, Jesus was simply tired and hoping to eat in peace. He didn't want to go and heal someone, leaving his food unattended and at

---

2 From the perspective of a Jew living in the 1st century in the Middle East, the world was divided into two groups of people--Jews, and everybody else. Those who were not Jewish were called Gentiles. It wasn't a bad thing to be a Gentile, however, Jewish people tended to avoid them.

the mercy of the local dog population who might try and eat it. This interpretation makes Jesus seem more human, albeit a little lazy.

But what if there's more to this story? What if this interaction is Jesus being ironic and playful? We know that Jesus is compassionate, but he was also quick-witted and clever. When he sees her act of humility he must know she is a woman of great faith. Perhaps he's testing her resolve?

When I picture the scene, I imagine this dialogue as playful banter between Jesus and the woman. When he says, "Let the children be fed first" (Mark 7:27), she throws it back to him by saying, "Yes Lord, but even the dogs under the table get the crumbs from the children" (v. 28). She's quick-witted too! Obviously, that impressed Jesus. I wonder if he laughed. I don't know if they did this back then or not, but maybe there was even a high-five between them. As if he set her up for it and she matched him word for word. Look at his response, "For this statement, go your way. The demon has left your daughter" (v. 29). He was impressed by her sly comeback and healed her daughter.

There are many more examples where English translations of Scripture prevent us from really being in on the joke. In Matthew 7, for example, Jesus is encouraging people not to judge each other. He says, "Why do you see the speck that is in your brother's eye, but do not notice the log that is in your own eye?" (Matthew 7:3).

Rather than imagining Jesus here as a somber professor, lecturing a group of his followers on a hillside, I visualize Jesus gesturing wildly as he acts out his teaching, like a first century version of Robin Williams. Think for a moment about what he is saying; it's a great visual illustration. He is saying, how in the world can you can pluck a microscopic piece of sawdust out of someone's eye when

> I VISUALIZE JESUS GESTURING WILDLY AS HE ACTS OUT HIS TEACHING, LIKE A FIRST CENTURY VERSION OF ROBIN WILLIAMS.

you have a 2x4 lodged in your own? It's a brilliant use of cynicism, irony, and hyperbole. It's clever and it's funny.

Later, Matthew records yet another great story in chapter 17. Jesus and his band of followers arrive in Capernaum. When they do, Peter is confronted by tax collectors, who want to know if Jesus is willing to pay the standard temple tax. For Jesus, this is a teachable moment. Jesus has no money, so he tells Peter, "go to the sea and cast a hook and take the first fish that comes up" (v. 27). Peter, a fisherman, does exactly what Jesus says, and guess what's in the fish's mouth? Money! Just enough to pay the tax collectors (v. 24-27).

Now, why didn't Jesus just do a Ben Kenobi move and wave his hand in the air saying, "we don't have to pay your temple tax." Or why not just conjure up a coin from thin air? Certainly, he could do that.

Over the years, I have heard plenty of Bible teachers ascribe theological meaning to this story. For example, the fish represents a Christian, the money in its mouth represents the gospel, and we are the mouthpieces to share the gospel with others.

While I suppose this interpretation is possible, in writing about this account, Matthew never states why Jesus pays the tax in this unique way. The only reason I can think of for Jesus asking Simon to pull money out of a fish's mouth is because it's funny—like an inside joke.

Please understand, I'm not saying Jesus was flippant. I'm not saying he was glib. I'm saying *he was real.* He was human. He had a compelling personality and people wanted to be around him. They never knew what he was going to do or say.

As you read through this book I hope you too will come to see Jesus as a real person. A person who is funny, tough, and rebellious. Someone who is all at once a teacher, friend, brother, creator, and most importantly, Messiah. And when you know more about him, you'll realize, you want to be around this Jesus too.

TWO

TOUGH JESUS

MORE THAN A ONE-DIMENSIONAL SAVIOR

"Life's not about how
hard of a hit you can give...
it's about how many you can take,
and still keep moving forward."

—Sylvester Stallone, Rocky Balboa

MANY PEOPLE HAVE GROWN UP to believe Jesus was an emaciated man who barely weighed 90 pounds. Just think of all those crucifixes you've seen—Jesus with a sallow face, protruding rib cage, bird-like arms—you get the picture. I once had a friend who was set to play Jesus in his church's upcoming passion play. He told me he had been skipping meals trying to get down to 130 pounds. Now that is one skinny Jesus!

Some people also think Jesus was a hippie. A kind of chai tea-drinking, Prius driving, peace symbol, tie-dye shirt wearing kind of guy. This Jesus is for peace and lets everyone do whatever they want as long as it's done in love. "Hey man," this Jesus says, "all you need is love." Oh wait, that was the Beatles.

Still others think Jesus was weak. A man who was bullied by the Pharisees. Since he couldn't defend himself against a bunch of Roman bullies he gave up and allowed himself to be beaten and then crucified.

So where do we get these ideas? TV and the internet have a role to play in this, of course, but we also get these notions from some of the worship songs we sing. Think about it. Have you ever been singing about Jesus, but you can't tell if you're singing to the Almighty Creator of the universe or to your on-again-off-again boyfriend or girlfriend?

The trouble is we've become comfortable with this weak, peace-loving Jesus. I mean, why not? What possible trouble could a man like that make for us? This feeble man is certainly someone who can be handled if not altogether ignored. He's a plaything, someone we can slip into our

> THE TROUBLE IS WE'VE
> BECOME COMFORTABLE
> WITH THIS WEAK, PEACE-
> LOVING JESUS.
> I MEAN, WHY NOT? WHAT
> POSSIBLE TROUBLE
> COULD A MAN LIKE THAT
> MAKE FOR US?

spiritual pocket when we don't want him or need him. Then on Sunday morning, we can take him out for a couple songs and a sermon.

If you have one of these inaccurate pictures of Jesus in your head right now, delete it. Close your eyes and imagine this inadequate version of Jesus standing in front of you. Now, notice a big red 'delete' button hovering just above his perfectly combed hair. Press it. Go ahead and delete him. We're going to build a new Jesus—the real Jesus—for you to picture from now on.

ACTION HERO

We have a guy in our church who is seven feet tall and built like a tank. He's a professional wrestler and bodybuilder and usually wears muscle shirts or tank tops. When I stand next to him I look like a kindergartener. He would be perfect to play the part of Goliath in Mel Gibson's next movie about the Bible. While he looks intimidating, he's also a super nice guy who cares deeply for his wife and child and serves in the community. Looks aren't always what they seem.

Would you believe me if I said Jesus looked like a tough guy? Okay, let me take some time to try and prove it to you. The prophet Isaiah prophesied about the coming Messiah around 700 years before Jesus was born. He said, "For he grew up before him like a young plant, and like a root out of dry ground; he had no form or majesty that we should look at him, and no beauty that we should desire him" (Isa. 53:2).

What does that mean? It means Jesus was a normal looking fellow. He was completely average. Not a tall statuesque man with long flowing hair. Not a guy with a permanent halo around his head. He didn't stand out from the crowd. You wouldn't have seen him and thought, *wow, that guy should be a model.*

The gospel writer, Mark, points out that Jesus was a carpenter (6:3). But the Greek word he used for carpenter is *tekton*, which can be translated more so to mean someone who works with wood, stone, or any kind of building material.

The Middle East is an arid climate with very few trees. So rather than seeing Jesus as a man who crafted tables and chairs out of wood, it's better to picture Jesus as someone who built things out of stone. As a matter of fact, it would not be a stretch to call Jesus something of a stonemason.

If you've ever seen a person that works with heavy materials like bricks and stone, then you know their hands are calloused. They develop thick muscular shoulders from carrying heavy loads on their back. Their legs become strong from lifting. This is a more accurate picture of what I believe Jesus looked like.

Jesus was just not the waif-like, white robe-wearing man we have been picturing all these years. He must have been strong and broad-chested, tanned by the sun from working outside. He was probably also shorter than you would expect. The average height of a man in the first century was only five feet two inches tall. That certainly changes the visual image of the man we worship.

Now, take that picture of Jesus and re-read John 2:13-16:

> The Passover of the Jews was at hand, and Jesus went up to Jerusalem. In the temple he found those who were selling oxen and sheep and pigeons, and the money-changers sitting there. And making a whip of cords, he drove them all out of the temple, with the sheep and oxen. And he poured out the coins of the money-changers and overturned their tables. And he told those who sold the pigeons, "Take these things away; do not make my Father's house a house of trade."

It would take a strong man to do this. The temple in Jerusalem was very large. Don't picture a few dozen people selling animals at a couple folding tables. Picture hundreds of people and lots of animals. Jesus ripped through the money-changers, overturning their tables and confronting those who were selling doves. It must have been pure chaos.

He also made a whip. A lot of people think that Jesus sort of went mad here, flipping out all the sudden. I don't read the text this way at all. When he saw that people in the temple were being swindled he had to do something, but he had no weapon. So, he sat down to make one. When was the last time you hand-crafted a whip? It had to take at least a few minutes. This was a premeditated assault. I wonder if he was looking at the money changers the whole time with this look that says, *just wait until I get done with this!*

When my Sunday School teachers told me this story I assumed that the money changers left the temple in an orderly fashion. But, now I think, why would they? I bet they resisted him. After all, his actions were costing them a lot of money. After the temple was cleared, the Pharisees confronted Jesus:

> So the Jews said to him, "What sign do you show us for doing these things?" Jesus answered them, "Destroy this temple, and in three days I will raise it up." The Jews then said, "It has taken forty-six years to build this temple, and will you raise it up in three days?" But he was speaking about the temple of his body (John 2:18-20).

The Pharisees demanded to know why Jesus thought he had the right to upset the system in such a way. When he tells them he can "rebuild this temple" they completely miss his point. Because Jesus was a builder, they thought he meant he would literally rebuild the Temple by hand. They didn't understand he was talking about his own body.

When I re-read this story with my new and more complete picture of Jesus, I don't see a weak and timid man at all. I see someone more like Arnold Schwarzenegger, Bruce Willis, or Chuck Norris.[3]

STRONG WORDS

Jesus spoke with authority. His words could not be ignored. Everything he said was important and weighty. He wasn't just visually tough, he was also verbally tough. Consider this story from Mark 4:36-39:

> And leaving the crowd, they took him with them in the boat, just as he was. And other boats were with him. And a great windstorm arose, and the waves were breaking into the boat, so that the boat was already filling. But he was in the stern, asleep on the cushion. And they woke him and said to him, "Teacher, do you not care that we are perishing?" And he awoke and rebuked the wind and said to the sea, "Peace! Be still!" And the wind ceased, and there was a great calm.

Whenever I used to read or hear this story I would picture Jesus napping in the back of the boat, a slight smile on his face. I used to think when Jesus was awakened by the disciples he yawned a bit and walked to the front of the boat, perched on the bow like that famous George Washington

---

3   Chuck Norris is a professing Christian. He's not just tough for knowing Karate. He's also tough because he stands up for his faith.

painting, and said (in a British accent, of course), "Peace, be still."

Go ahead and erase those images from your head because they're not accurate either. Instead, imagine the chaos of a terrible storm—bad enough the disciples think the boat is about to go under. They must have been yelling to Jesus just to be heard over the wind.

Now, I don't know about you, but the last time someone woke me up by yelling at me I was a little grumpy. Considering the Bible says Jesus "rebuked" the wind and waves, tells me he may have been a little put out as well. A more modern translation might say that Jesus woke up and yelled at the waves and wind, "Enough already, shut up!"

The Greek word Mark uses to describe Jesus's tone is *epitimaō*, which means to speak from a place of authority and honor—like the way your Dad speaks when he's had enough of the kids in the back seat of the car. My Dad is a pretty quiet guy and he only raised his voice to me on a couple occasions while I was growing up. However, when he did it would create a sense of fear in me. Not bad fear, but good fear—respect. Once, when I had been disrespectful during a church service he looked me straight in the eye and said, "We'll deal with this when we get home." I knew exactly what he meant. When he said that to me I'm pretty sure I needed a change of pants. It was the same with Jesus. When he spoke to the wind and waves that day, the sea had to change its pants!

Jesus spoke with this kind of authority because he is the creator of the universe. His words shaped the cosmos in every way. Many people think the voice of Jesus speaks out against them, rebuking them. Perhaps you feel this way too. Maybe you feel like the voice of Jesus is critical of you. But 1 John 2:1 paints a different picture. Jesus actually speaks on your behalf: "My little children, I am writing these things to you so that you may not sin. But if anyone does sin, we have an advocate with the Father, Jesus Christ the righteous."

How does this make you feel? I hope it makes you feel great. Think of it—the voice of the man who woke up and calmed the wind and waves with a few words doesn't speak against you—he speaks for you. He is an advocate on your behalf to God.

TOUGH ENOUGH

Once I had an abscess on the bottom of my foot. It was incredibly painful. I went to the doctor and after one look he said, "Well, we are going to need to cut that open."

I gulped, "Cut it open? Isn't there another way? Like, with medicine or something?"

"Nope," he said, pulling on a glove and letting it snap. "We have to relieve the pressure and drain the infected puss."

Without question, this was the most painful thing I have ever experienced. I had hoped there was another way to take care of the abscess, but the scalpel was the only option for relief.

Jesus experienced a lot of pain too. In Luke's gospel we are treated to the special perspective of a doctor. We know Luke was a physician (Col. 4:14) and one of his goals in writing his gospel account was to share intricate or compelling details of Jesus's life, some of which are not included in the other three gospels (Matthew, Mark, and John).

For example, in Luke 22 he tells the incredible story of Jesus's prayer in the garden of Gethsemane. Like Matthew and Mark, Luke shares about Jesus praying and asking the cup be taken from him (v. 42). Jesus hoped there was another way to deliver the universe from sin besides going to the cross.

However, Luke includes an incredible detail involving a condition medically known as *hematidrosis*. This is when someone literally sweats blood. When Jesus prayed to the Father, he was in such agony over the coming crucifixion Luke says, "his sweat became like great drops of blood falling down to the ground" (v. 44b).

Some see this as a weakness, as if Jesus was so afraid of torture and being nailed to a wooden cross he was begging God for a way out. But praying for another option is not cowardice or weakness. It's courage. We can see this at the conclusion of Jesus's prayer when he said, "not my will, but yours, be done" (v. 42b). Bravely, he put his life in his Father's hands.

If you watch too many movies about Jesus or listen to popular songs you might get the idea Jesus was also a fragile man. Popular songs have conveyed this idea in recent times. One of my least favorite songs is "Above All," performed by Michael W. Smith. The lyrics say, "Like a rose, trampled on the ground, you took the fall and thought of me, above all."

I don't mind the idea that Jesus took our place on the cross, but I can't stand the image of Jesus as a helpless victim—tossed aside and trampled on the ground.

No one murdered Jesus. At least not without his consent. No one had the power to take his life from him. He willingly and purposefully gave himself over to the ridicule, abuse, and torture of the cross. He was clear about this in the gospel of John where he said, "I lay down my life that I may take it up again. No one takes it from me, but I lay it down of my own accord" (10:17b-18).

Jesus was crucified because he allowed himself to be crucified. At any time during the hours leading up to his death he could have called it off. Who could blame him if he had?

> NO ONE MURDERED JESUS. AT LEAST NOT WITHOUT HIS CONSENT. NO ONE HAD THE POWER TO TAKE HIS LIFE FROM HIM. HE WILLINGLY AND PURPOSEFULLY GAVE HIMSELF OVER TO THE RIDICULE, ABUSE, AND TORTURE OF THE CROSS.

Crucifixion is an intentionally torturous and painful way to die, and the Romans had perfected the art of killing in this way. Crucifixion involved several steps. First, Jesus was flogged by a whip which had shards of bone and metal bits tied into the leather thongs. This beating would have been brutal enough to shred his skin and muscle, down to the bone underneath. After this, he was ordered to carry his own cross to a hill known as Golgotha. There, his punishment and torture would be on display for all. For the Romans, the goal was not only to kill someone, but to shame them—to put them on display. It was incredibly painful, and it was incredibly degrading.

Among scholars, there is much debate about whether Jesus was nailed to the cross, or just tied to it. The Romans used both methods when crucifying their victims. However, there is clear evidence that Jesus endured the pain of being nailed to the cross. The gospel of John records Thomas doubting the risen Jesus by saying, "Unless I see in his hands the mark of the nails, and place my finger into the mark of the nails...I will never believe" (John 20:25).

After being whipped, beaten, and nailed to the cross, Jesus hung in agony for six hours. He endured the intense pain and persevered through the torture from 9:00 am in the morning to 3:00 pm in the afternoon.

Would a weak Jesus been able to withstand that kind of torture? The fragile, pacifist Jesus would have given up far earlier. But the visually tough, verbally tough, and mentally tough Jesus showed his strength at that moment. Evidence of this extraordinary tenacity comes from the testimony of a Roman centurion who was on hand to supervise his death. Centurions were professional executioners and witnessed countless people die during crucifixions. The courage Jesus displayed during his death caused the centurion to state, "Surely this man was the Son of God!" (Mark 15:39). Now that is tough.

A man that tough is very compelling. A man like that cannot be ignored. People will not follow a weakling or someone who shows no strength of character. But people will follow a man of integrity. They will follow a man who has strength of character, mind, and body.

Jesus was this man. His courage, grit, and tenacity can't be ignored. Each person must confront the reality of this new picture of Jesus. And each person must decide whether or not to allow this Jesus to be the leader in their life.

What does your picture of Jesus look like? How do you see him? Has the picture you have had of him in your mind changed at all? Are you still imagining a sallow-faced, sweet-smelling Savior, or are you looking up to a man with the power and strength to defeat death on a cross?

I encourage you to forget the lesser Jesus and start looking at the tough one. It makes such a big difference when you do. Now, when you read a story in the Bible you'll understand why people were so drawn to him and why others were so repelled. When you hear sermons about him you'll recognize his tenacity and grit. And when you pray to him, you'll know he has the strength to deliver on his promises and carry you through all of life's challenges.

THREE
REBEL JESUS

MORE THAN A ONE-DIMENSIONAL SAVIOR

"It takes nothing
to join the crowd.
It takes everything
to stand alone."

—Hans F. Hansen

THE FIRST TIME I SAW the movie *Rebel Without a Cause*, I was blown away. The film was made in 1955 and starred James Dean and Natalie Wood. It's a classic.

One of the reasons the film resonated with me was because James Dean was so cool. He was handsome, brooding, and misunderstood. Plus, he had that jean jacket. To me, he was on another level of cool.

In the film, James portrays a high school kid heading in the wrong direction. He's new in town, in trouble with the law, and he can't make friends. It was a groundbreaking movie because it was one of the first films to portray a troubled group of teens as lead characters. They were rebelling against their parents' control and against society's preconceived ideas about young people. I remember feeling a kinship with the teens in the movie, even though I didn't have much cause to rebel against anything.

But Jesus did. He rebelled against a lot. Are you thinking, *hmmm, that doesn't sound right*? Maybe when you hear the word 'rebel' you don't think "Son of God." But really, Jesus was extremely rebellious.

Don't get me wrong, Jesus was perfectly obedient to the will of his Father and to his mission on the earth. He obeyed his parents and followed the teaching of the law with precision. But he was rebellious in a spiritual way. This caused the religious leaders of the day to view him as a troublemaker.

The main difference between Jesus and James Dean (besides the awesome jean jacket), was that Jesus *had* a cause. An important one. And no one could stand in the way of that cause.

CONFRONTING CORRUPT LEADERSHIP

In 1887, the British historian Lord Acton said, "Power tends to corrupt, and absolute power corrupts absolutely."[4] This has been true for millennia. In the first century there was no shortage of spiritual leaders, however, many of them were corrupt. There were numerous leaders that tangled with Jesus during his life, but a few stand out more than others.

The first were the Sadducees. They were part of the religious ruling class and were powerful and rich. They believed in the books of Moses, also known as "The Law," as authoritative (Genesis-Deuteronomy), but they were far more interested in pleasing the Roman government than in helping people follow God. They were tasked with running the affairs of the Temple in Jerusalem, but their goals were primarily political.

The second group were the Pharisees. They ran the affairs of the synagogue, which put them in more contact with the regular people. Like the Sadducees, they too followed the books of Moses as law, but they also believed a traditional interpretation of the law should be followed on the same level as the Bible. More on that later.

---

4 Christopher Lazarski, *Power Tends to Corrupt: Lord Acton's Study of Liberty* (DeKalb:Northern Illinois University Press, 2012),

In both cases, the Sadducees and the Pharisees, used Scripture and tradition to control people. While tasked with controlling the temple and synagogue, overseeing religious festivals and interpreting the Scriptures, they worked more in spite of people rather than on behalf of them. It is safe to say their goal was to control God's people, not help them or lead them.

Jesus debated with the Pharisees on a number of occasions. Once, after he had a heated conversation with them regarding his lordship he turned to his disciples as well as those who had been following him and said, "The scribes and the Pharisees sit on Moses' seat, so do and observe whatever they tell you, but not the works they do. For they preach, but do not practice" (Matt. 23:2-3).

In other words, he was saying they talk the talk, but they don't walk the walk. When Jesus said this, the Pharisees were still standing nearby. No doubt they heard every single word. In the verses that follow in Matthew 23, Jesus preached a blazing sermon called, "The Seven Woes" (v. 13-39) where he detailed every single way the Pharisees had fallen short of true, heartfelt faith in God.

If you think Jesus is too harsh remember what's at stake. In verse 13, he tells the crowd that the Pharisees, "shut the kingdom of heaven in people's faces." These religious leaders were doing more harm than good. Jesus saw they were a barrier to the kingdom of heaven. Plus, if they did convert an individual, Jesus said they were destined to become "twice as much a child of hell" (v. 15) as the Pharisees. Those are very strong words.

Perhaps you can relate when Jesus talks about these derelict teachers leading people astray. If you've grown up in the church, you might even be thinking of a certain leader—maybe a pastor or Sunday school teacher that used their power or influence to make you feel shame about your faith.

As I grew up in the church during the 80's I recall a lot of leaders using guilt as a tool to keep church-goers in check. While it's hardly an isolated incident anymore, I can remember having a youth pastor that frequently talked about the danger in inappropriate sexual activity. He was passionate about making sure we all knew how dangerous premarital sex was.

Eventually, we found out he had been having an illicit affair with a woman who was not his wife. He was fired, left the church, and, in the wake of the controversy, our tiny youth group was destroyed. We all looked at each other—speechless to describe the level of betrayal we felt. He was living out different principles from what he taught.

Of course, no one's perfect. We understand that. However, the big problem for Jesus is that the Pharisees and other teachers in the religious ruling class had expectations of their followers they were not willing to keep themselves. That's his point.

If you find yourself in a church or spiritual community where the leaders use guilt and spiritual manipulation to force you into following, be careful. That's a big red flag. Many of those leaders have very little accountability or oversight. Worse, they often surrounded themselves with sycophants—people who are unwilling to be honest and confront their destructive leadership.

GOD HAS LEFT THE BUILDING

I attended a small, Christian college that had lots and lots of rules to follow. One of those rules stated that we were required to wear a tie to church on Sunday. Since I considered myself a bit of a rebel, I decided that I didn't want to wear a tie. I was pulled aside by the Resident Assistant (RA), who reminded me about the rule. He said, "Like it or not, you must wear a tie to church on Sunday. Don't let me catch you next Sunday without one or I'll be forced to write you up."

"Okay," I said, assuring him I would have one on next week.

The following Sunday he bumped into me at church and noticed that I wasn't wearing a tie. As he began his mini-lecture on the rules I told him to wait. I reached *into* my shirt and pulled my tie out for him to see. Yes, I was wearing a tie, but it was not visible because I had it on under my shirt! I said, "You never told me that I had to wear it on the *outside* of my clothes."

Looking back, I realize my actions were immature and selfish. I was content to follow the letter of the law, but not the spirit of the law. I followed the rules, but I missed the whole point.

Bono, the lead singer of the popular band, U2, once said, "Religion to me is almost like when God leaves—and people devise a set of rules to fill the space."[5]

This quote had a big impact on my life after I heard it. The reason it affected me so deeply was because this was exactly the way a lot of my church experience had been. Growing up, I often felt like being a Christian was just about following a long list of "do-nots." Similarly, I've had many conversations with men and women that have grown up in various denominations that feel the same way.

Jesus rebelled against a broken religious system that placed rules and regulations above the spiritual needs of the community. Leaders like the Pharisees and Sadducees loved spiritual rules and regulations. You can see why they didn't get along with Jesus; he threatened their status quo.

The rules and regulations they were so fond of did come from the Old Testament in the Bible. If you were to count up all the rules from the 5 books of the Law (Genesis, Exodus, Leviticus, Numbers, and Deuteronomy) you get a total of 613 rules, or commandments. However, in typical human fashion, corrupt teachers had taken it upon themselves to add all kinds of decrees and ordinances to the Law—making it complicated and impossible to follow. They did this in an effort to explain the Law. This explanation eventually became known as the *Mishnah*. It was like a companion

---

5   Steve Stockman, *Walk On: The Spiritual Journey of U2* (Orlando:Relevant Books 2005),

guide to the Old Testament law, compiled by a group of rabbis.[6]

In the gospel of Mark 2:23-28, the Pharisees accused Jesus and his disciples of breaking the fourth commandment, which says we are to "honor the Sabbath, keep it holy" (Exod. 20:8). Jesus and his disciples had walked through a wheat field on a Saturday, and as they did each disciple plucked a few heads of grains to eat. This was a common custom and was not considered stealing.[7]

The Pharisees saw a prime opportunity to accuse Jesus and the disciples of mistreating the Sabbath and breaking Old Testament Law. However, the Pharisees should have known the point of the fourth commandment has very little to do with sampling a couple kernels of grain as you walk along a path. The point of God's command has to do with his people resting one day per week—for physical and spiritual renewal. Picking kernels of grain is certainly not going to prevent anyone from this.

In response, Jesus reminded them about a famous story, also from the Old Testament, concerning David and the bread of the Presence.

During this time, David was on the run from king Saul, who wanted to kill him. When David and his men took refuge in the temple they were hungry and the only bread available was called, "the bread of the Presence" (1

---

6   The Mishnah is still available for purchase today. The book is almost 1,000 pages long.

7   The Old Testament law (Lev. 19:9-10) specified farmers should intentionally leave grain on the edges of their fields so the poor and those traveling could eat.

Sam. 21:6) which was forbidden, except for priests, during sacrifice. Given the urgent nature of David's predicament, the priest allowed him and his men to eat the special bread (v. 1-6).

The Pharisees knew this story well and Jesus made his point clearly: Sometimes rules are more like guidelines, and often, the spirit of the law is more important than the letter of the law.

Jesus finished his reprimand by telling the Pharisees the "sabbath is made for men, not men for the sabbath" (Mark 2:27). Then he said, "So the Son of Man is lord even of the Sabbath" (v. 28). If he'd had a microphone in his hand, this would have been the moment he would have dropped it and walked off stage.

How many times have we been led to believe the letter of the law is more important than the spirit of it? And how often have we placed this burden on ourselves? Rather than follow God and pursue holiness for the sheer joy and pleasure of pleasing God, we try to manage a giant list of do-nots, thinking if we step out of line God will be angry with us and ready to strike us down with one of those lightning bolts he keeps handy.

Over the last twenty-years of studying the Scripture, I've come to realize the Bible isn't a big list of do-nots, it's actually just a couple of "dos."

When the teachers of law tried to trap Jesus by asking him which Old Testament law was the most important, he had an answer for them. He told them the first and greatest commandment was, "You shall love the Lord your

God with all your heart and with all your soul and with all your mind" (Mark 12:30). Then he followed with a second commandment (they had only asked for one). He said, "The second is this:

> OVER THE LAST TWENTY-YEARS OF STUDYING THE SCRIPTURE, I'VE COME TO REALIZE THE BIBLE ISN'T A BIG LIST OF DO-NOTS, IT'S ACTUALLY JUST A COUPLE OF "DOS."

'You shall love your neighbor as yourself.' There is no other commandment greater than these" (v. 31).

Jesus replaced 613 do-nots with two dos. Two! It's simple: if you follow these commandments—loving God with all you have, and loving your neighbor like yourself—you won't have to worry about breaking any of those other rules. Amazing.

WHAT HAVE YOU DONE FOR ME LATELY?

Jesus rebelled against corrupt spiritual leaders and against a broken religious system. He also rebelled against short-sighted people with selfish assumptions about Jesus. There were plenty of people who were following Jesus because of what they could get from him. They weren't interested in his mission and vision to save the world from sin, they were interested in achieving reputation, power, and even food.

One of Jesus's more famous miracles is documented in the gospel of John chapter six. Jesus took a few fish and loaves from a young boy's lunch and made them into a feast for more than 5,000 people. Later that evening, he and his disciples went to the other side of the sea from where they had been (Mark 1-13, 16-21).

Then it says the people got into boats and followed him across the water (v. 24). Jesus knew what they wanted—more food! (v. 26). Their assumption was temporal and selfish. While Jesus had been talking about his coming kingdom of faith, forgiveness, and healing, they couldn't get their minds off of their rumbling stomachs (v. 26-35).

Even a few of Jesus's disciples had selfish assumptions. They knew Jesus was powerful, and they wanted some of that power too. Mark's gospel recounts a time when James and his brother John approached Jesus with a special request. They asked, "Grant us to sit, one at your right hand and one at your left, in your glory" (10:37). Jesus didn't actually turn down their request, he just said the decision was not his to make. However, he rebelled against their selfish request. Rather than grant their wish outright, Jesus took advantage of a teachable moment for the disciples. Jesus told them true leadership is not about what you can get for yourself, but what you can give to others. He reminded them the world views leadership as having a position of honor, but God views leadership as an opportunity to serve (v. 43-44). Just before his death, Jesus came into Jerusalem one last time and he did so in spectacular fashion. All four gospels, Matthew, Mark, Luke, and John[8], detail the way Jesus arrived in the

---

8   Matthew 21:1-11, Mark 11:1-11, Luke 19:28-44, and John 12:12-19

city that day. He was riding on a donkey. At first glance this seems strange and the opposite of powerful. But, when you realize that this special entry into the city is a direct fulfillment of the prophecy in Zechariah 9:9, the picture comes into full focus.[9]

By arriving in Jerusalem on a donkey, it was like Jesus was declaring, *Yes, I am your king. I am the one here to rescue you and bring peace.* The people loved it. They wanted a king and needed a leader to deliver them from the oppression of the occupying Roman government.

But again, Jesus rebelled against this notion. It was far too short-sighted. Jesus was ready to fulfill every one of the prophecies mentioned by Zechariah, but not only here on this earth and not only during his short lifetime. The peace he intended to bring was not political, but *spiritual.* His goal was not to deliver the people from the oppression of the Romans but from the oppression of sin. This was not what they had in mind, but like always, what Jesus wants for us is better than what *we* want for us.

When we read the scriptures, it's easy to portray many of Jesus's followers of being short-sighted and selfish. However, it's a good idea to look inside ourselves too. Have you ever asked yourself, "What do I want from Jesus? Is it just what I want, or is it what he wants for me?" Do we only want the things that make us comfortable and content, or are we willing to accept a more difficult path?

---

9 The prophecy written by Zechariah declares the deliverer of Israel will not only ride into Jerusalem on a donkey, but will bring peace to the nations.

I think this is one of the reasons many believers exit the church and eventually give up on faith. They want to be comfortable. They want Jesus to make life easy. And when these expectations aren't met, things start to get uncomfortable, or look different from their own ideas of what they want from God, they give up and leave. Unfortunately, a lot of the time, those expectations are shaped by the spiritual leaders in their life who failed to teach them the full cost of following Jesus. The rich, full, but not always easy or comfortable, life with Jesus as Lord.

I have heard TV evangelists, Sunday School teachers, and preachers tell their congregations and classes how Jesus wants to make their life better, and give them all they need. I've heard promises of a happiness beyond compare and unspeakable joy to those who follow Christ. While all of that is true, it must be placed into the context of what it truly means to follow Jesus.

Jesus calls his followers to a high-standard of self-sacrifice. He plainly acknowledges the fact there will be suffering for those who believe in him. He never promised a perfect life. To the contrary, he predicted trouble for his people— knowing they would face great opposition from non-believers and from the enemy, Satan.

In John 17, Jesus prays a surprising and magnificent prayer. He asks God to give strength to all the believers, knowing they would be hated and mistreated just because they bear the name of Christ (v. 20-26).

In many ways, having the strength to withstand mistreatment in the name of Jesus is about being rebellious like he was. He stood up to a broken system, corrupt leadership, and even selfish people. If we are to follow Jesus, then we must rebel as he did. It's good to be a rebel when you have a cause.

FOUR
TEACHER JESUS

MORE THAN A ONE-DIMENSIONAL SAVIOR

"The mediocre teacher tells.
The good teacher explains.
The superior teacher demonstrates.
The great teacher inspires."

—William Ward

MY ALL-TIME FAVORITE TEACHER WAS a guy named Mr. Carter. I think I liked him because he bucked the system and worked hard to make learning fun. He did a lot of funny and crazy things. For example, one day in 1981, he showed up to class wearing a spacesuit and wheeling a TV into the room. He said, "We won't be doing any classwork today so put your books away. Today you get to watch history in the making." After he turned out the lights and flipped on the TV, we all watched the very first space shuttle land. I'll never forget that.

You probably already know that Jesus made a great impact as a teacher, but did you know Jesus was the greatest teacher that ever lived? I say that with confidence because sheer numbers prove it. As of 2010, nearly 2.2 billion people described themselves as Christians. At the time of this study there were 6.9 billion people on the earth. This means that a third of all people recognize Jesus's teachings as life-changing and true.[10]

When you understand that Jesus only taught for three years, just 36 months, you can see the impact he's had on the world as a teacher is unrivaled. No one else in history has been able to make this kind of impact so quickly.

However, sometimes we can take his teaching for granted. Maybe it's because we are so familiar with it. Even if you didn't grow up attending church you've heard principles like

---

10   Bill Chappell, "World's Muslim Population Will Surpass Christians This Century, Pew Says," NPR, http://www.npr.org/sections/thetwo-way/2015/04/02/397042004/muslim-population-will-surpass-christians-this-century-pew-says (accessed June 2, 2017).

"Do unto others as you would have them do unto you" (Luke 6:31). Famously known as The Golden Rule, we are so accustomed to it we hardly think twice about how revolutionary this kind of idea was in the first century. Throughout history, people haven't always cared about the feelings and needs of others. Even though there is still a lot of pain and suffering in the world, principles like The Golden Rule have made a marked difference in the way we treat each other since Jesus lived.

In his gospel, Matthew described the reaction people had after Jesus taught about several topics, ranging from prayer and philanthropy to wealth and anxiety. He wrote that the people were astonished because Jesus taught with a certain authority they hadn't experienced before (Luke 7:28). Later, Matthew says they marveled at his teaching (Luke 22:22).

People were excited to hear what Jesus had to say. They followed him around to the point where it became difficult for him to move (Luke 5:1). It was like they couldn't get enough of him, of his ideas and principles.

What made Jesus such a great teacher? Why did so many people follow him then, and why do so many people still follow him today?

FOR THE PEOPLE

Jesus spoke directly to the hearts and the needs of the people. He spoke the truth and he was relevant. What he said meant something to the people and it mattered. He didn't dwell on lofty spiritual principles that were too difficult for people to understand, instead he made things simple and got to the heart of the matter.

Right from the beginning of his public ministry, Jesus was a relevant teacher. He had just come back from being in the wilderness for 40 days when he went to the synagogue in Nazareth, his hometown. Luke says he stood up was handed a scroll to read. He unrolled it and read:

> The Spirit of the Lord is upon me, because he has anointed me to proclaim good news to the poor. He has sent me to proclaim liberty to the captives and recovering of sight to the blind, to set at liberty those who are oppressed, to proclaim the year of the Lord's favor (Luke 4:18-19, as quoted from Isa. 61).

This was no ordinary reading. It was prophecy come to life. Centuries earlier Isaiah had written these words, with the inspiration of the Spirit, about Jesus. Talk about a *meta-moment*! Here's Jesus, as the Messiah, reading a scroll, about the Messiah.

What is most significant about the way Jesus taught was He custom-tailored each message for exactly those who needed to hear it. For example, to the poor he says he has a message of good news. What do the poor need more than good news? To those imprisoned he promises liberty. What does a captive dream about more than freedom? To the blind he proclaims sight. To the oppressed he declares deliverance.

The list goes on. Jesus gently offers grace to those who need it, every time.

Jesus was also relevant because he joined people in their day to day lives. While many teachers spent their time only teaching in the synagogue, Jesus taught from all kinds of places. He taught from the bows of boats, on hills, in houses, and while he walked. It seems like wherever he was there was always a group of people thirsty to hear his instruction.

Not only did he go to the people, but he spoke their language. While many of the educated and elite teachers of the day were apt to speak in a traditional Hebrew dialect or even classical Greek, Jesus used the common language, Aramaic. This may account for why people were so astonished by the depth and quality of his teaching. While he sounded just like a "regular Joe," his principles were profound, new, and engaging.

CREATIVITY COUNTS

In the church where I serve I have the opportunity to teach from the Bible about 45 times per year. I've been the lead teaching pastor for about 10 years, which means I've given almost 500 sermons! Of all the teaching I've done the sermons that are most memorable to people are the ones where I used props, visual illustrations, or other creative measures. For example, one time I asked a couple of talented artists in our church to paint a picture during my teaching.

I told the story of the woman at the well and they painted the story live.

Another time, I preached a whole sermon while handcuffed to illustrate being bound by the law. Once, I even cooked a whole meal, complete with steak, veggies, and sides live on stage while I spoke. I then invited a few people to eat the meal to illustrate the idea that mature believers eat food and not milk. When it comes to communicating, creativity counts.

When Jesus taught people he was very creative. Most of the time he taught with stories, which created a powerful visual for those listening. As the gospel of Matthew says, "All these things Jesus said to the crowds in parables; indeed, he said nothing to them without a parable" (Matt. 13:34). Story-based teaching is powerful because it taps into people's natural interest in other people. One time he told the story of a woman who had lost a precious coin (Luke 15:8-10). Another time he talked about a man who had been robbed and beaten (Luke 10:25-37). Jesus used common, ordinary situations to capture the attention of his listeners because everybody is interested in hearing a good story they can personally relate to.

Jesus also knew that people learn visually. According to a recent study by the University of Alabama, two out of three people are visual learners.[11] This means it is easier for certain

---

11   TJ McCue, Why Infographics Rule, Forbes Magazine. https://www.forbes.com/sites/tjmccue/2013/01/08/what-is-an-infographic-and-ways-to-make-it-go-viral (accessed Aug 13, 2017).

people to understand the point of a story if the teaching involves something they can picture in their mind.

The stories Jesus told often involved visual illustrations and hyperbole. One of the most well-known examples of this happens in Luke 18:18-25 when Jesus encounters a wealthy young man.

The man asks Jesus what it takes to have eternal life and Jesus tells him that he should keep the 10 commandments. When the man tells Jesus that he has kept all of them since the day he was born, Jesus immediately knows his heart. It's simply not possible to keep every command perfectly. So Jesus tells him to sell everything he owns, distribute it to the poor, and then become a disciple. The young man decides that is too much for him to do. He had a lot of money and he was not willing to part with it.

In response, Jesus remarks, "It is easier for a camel to go through the eye of a needle than for a rich person to enter the kingdom of God" (v. 25). This is a powerful use of hyperbole, imagery, and comedy. His audience would have immediately realized the point of his teaching by visualizing the impassibility of a large animal fitting through such a small hole.

A HOUSE BUILT ON ROCK

My wife has been a math and science teacher to fifth graders since 1992. She's very good at what she does. Her kids love coming to school and learning. She's creative and interesting to listen to, and very passionate about her subject matter too. But she wouldn't be a very good teacher if no one learned anything. It would be terrible if the kids exited her class only knowing the same information as when they entered. What a waste that would be. No, my wife's students leave fifth grade with changed mindsets about math and science. Kids leave smarter than when they arrived. This is the most important sign of a good teacher.

Jesus was a good teacher for a lot of reasons. Obviously, he was relevant and creative, but he also demanded change from people. Teaching is a two-way street. The teacher teaches but the students must do more than listen; they must change.

In Matthew 7, Jesus illustrated this expertly. Using all of his creativity and relevancy, he painted a picture of two men; each one building a house. One man decided to build his house on a good foundation—solid rock. The other decided to construct his house on sand. Choosing a good foundation to build on was important because soon a great storm came and tested both of the houses. In the end, only one remained standing—the one built on rock (v. 24-27).

The point of Jesus's story was simple. If you hear the words of the master teacher and you follow them, you will be like the man who built his house on the rock. But if you hear the teaching of Jesus and do nothing, your house will not last.

Of course, Jesus isn't really talking about houses or buildings, he is talking about life. Many people fail to realize how powerful the message of Jesus Christ really is. It's life changing on a spiritual level, of course, but it makes a lot of sense now, here on earth too. His teachings about love, forgiveness, worry, and money will make a big difference in your life if you choose to follow them. You are the only one who can make the choice for yourself.

This is why it's so important that we as believers take an active role every time we read the Bible and every time we hear someone teach from it. We must absorb the teaching and strive to make changes in our own lives. This requires being intentional in our learning, asking questions and challenging ourselves during the learning process. The best two questions to ask while you're reading the Bible are: 1) *What do I need to know?* and 2) *Do I need to change anything?*

This is not about legalism and following a list of rules. This is about allowing the words of Christ to penetrate our hearts so deeply change happens. Then, when the storms of life approach we know we are standing on a firm foundation, given to us by our Great Teacher, ready to handle anything that comes our way.

WE MUST ABSORB THE TEACHING AND STRIVE TO MAKE CHANGES IN OUR OWN LIVES.

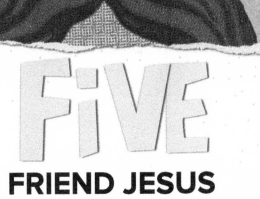

FIVE

FRIEND JESUS

MORE THAN A ONE-DIMENSIONAL SAVIOR

"Friendship has
always belonged
to the core of
my spiritual journey."

—Henri Nouwen

I HAVE SOME REALLY CLOSE friends I've known for most of my life. Whenever we get together we always find ways to compete with one another. I guess it's a guy thing. We have contests involving the silliest things - video games, board games, shooting hoops, golf, and even who is the best at shuffling cards. It's kind of silly but we've been competing since we were young. Now that we're not so young anymore we still find it entertaining.

However, the reason I like spending time with my friends is not because of the games we play—it's because they are *good* friends. They don't judge me. If I have a problem they will listen to me. They find ways to encourage me and if we ever have a disagreement they are more than willing to forgive me. That's what friends do.

Jesus was a friend like that. That's why so many people were drawn to him. He took chances on people, avoiding judgement and choosing to show kindness and gentleness instead. He was friendly to different kinds of people too. The kind of people most folks would avoid.

A WEE LITTLE MAN

I grew up in church and one of my favorite Bible stories was about a little guy named Zacchaeus. There's even a song about him. It's a cute little song that focuses on the fact Zacchaeus was a short fellow. The song does a good job of explaining why Zacchaeus climbed up a tree. Since Jesus was heading his way he wanted to see him, but the crowds were too tall. So he climbed up in a tree. But Zacchaeus' most important trait was not that he was short but that he was a tax collector and that he was rich.

This is one of those places in the scripture it's important to know a little historical background. When Jesus was on earth all of Palestine was under the rule of Rome. As an occupying force, Rome collected taxes from the Jewish people. Lots of taxes. The Jewish people paid income tax, import tax, export tax, grain tax, wine tax, sales tax, and property tax.

The Romans rarely collected these taxes directly from the Jewish people. Instead, they sold the rights to collect taxes to the highest bidder. In the case of Zacchaeus, he had won the right to take taxes from his countrymen.

Zacchaeus was a Jew and because he worked for the Romans he was a hated individual. Tax collectors were viewed as traitors and thieves. In many cases they took more than they were entitled to, and when they did the Romans looked the other way.

Luke 19:1-8 records Jesus going into Jericho and looking up into a tree to address Zacchaeus. He said to him, "Zacchaeus, hurry and come down, for I must stay at your house today" (v. 5).

Of course, many onlookers were outraged to think Jesus would spend time with a man like Zacchaeus—a known turncoat and thief. After all, why would the Son of God associate with someone that was so hated?

The response of Zacchaeus may give us some indication of why Jesus was interested in him. Zacchaeus replied,

"Lord, the half of my goods I give to the poor. And if I have defrauded anyone of anything, I restore it fourfold" (v. 8).[12]

Zacchaeus had an instant change of heart. He responded to Jesus with repentance. He was ready to change, he just needed someone to believe in him.

But notice that Jesus took a chance on him. Jesus didn't say, "Zacchaeus, I'm coming to your house today *if* you give everyone's money back." No, he befriended him first, just because. Jesus did that often and it left his enemies befuddled.

LIVING WATER

Jesus was a friend to women. That doesn't sound like too much of a big deal, but for the time it was. In the first century, women were regarded as far less important than men. Truthfully, it is still this way in most of the undeveloped world, even sometimes in the developed world too.

The gospel writer, Luke, adds an interesting detail in chapter 8 where he makes it a point to highlight women among the followers and disciples of Jesus. He writes, "And the twelve were with him, and also some women who had been healed of evil spirits and infirmities: Mary, called Magdalene, from whom seven demons had gone out, and

---

12   It is significant Zacchaeus decided to repay any amount stolen by a factor of four. In the Old Testament, if a thief was caught he was to repay any stolen items by four. This notion reveals the fact Zacchaeus had indeed stolen from the people and was willing to submit to the Old Testament law to make things right.

Joanna, the wife of Chuza, Herod's household manager, and Susanna, and many others, who provided for them out of their means" (v. 1b-3).

It was taboo for a Rabbi to associate too much with women. But Jesus was willing to befriend anyone who needed healing and salvation, regardless of their gender or reputation. One such example occurs in the gospel of John, chapter 4.

Jesus was on his way to Galilee and to get there he had to pass through Samaria. Usually, Jews would go around Samaria because the Jews and the Samaritans did not like each other. It's a long story that goes back several centuries.[13] However, Jesus went straight through Samaria.

On the way, he became tired and thirsty and stopped by a well. The disciples went ahead into town to gather supplies. While he was at the well he encountered a woman who was there to draw water. According to the gospel writer, we know she came to the well around noon. This is a subtle hint as to what kind of reputation the woman had. Most women would have drawn their water early in the day. We can make a reasonable assumption that because she was there later in the day she was hoping to avoid the regular group of women at the well.

At the well, Jesus asked her for a drink. She was surprised by his request because ordinarily Jews and Samaritans didn't

---

13   The disagreement between Jews and Samaritans started when the Assyrians conquered Israel in 722 B.C. and replaced its citizens with foreigners. Those foreigners intermarried with the remnants from the northern kingdom of Israel and introduced idol worship to the territory.

socialize. But again, the playful and sometimes mischievous nature of Jesus is visible when he says, "If you knew the gift of God, and who it is that is saying to you, 'Give me a drink,' you would have asked him and he would have given you living water" (v. 10).

There's a few things going on here in between the lines of the text. First, she was blown away he would even talk to her. The difference in nationalities should have been enough reason for him to ignore her. Secondly, he's a man and she's a woman. It was highly unusual and inappropriate for a single man to be alone with a woman in such a secluded place. It could be considered especially scandalous considering her dubious reputation. She had been through a total of five husbands and was now living with a man to whom she was not married. When the disciples came back they were amazed Jesus had been speaking with her (v. 27). Their surprise doesn't come from the fact that Jesus is talking about living water, it comes from the fact that Jesus is alone with a woman of questionable character.

So why does Jesus put his reputation at risk? Simple, he is a friend to those who need a friend. He is a savior to those who need saving. He reaches out to people despite their circumstances and reputation.

In the end, this woman recognized Jesus as the true Messiah. We know this because she immediately began spreading the good news about Jesus to the rest of her town (v. 29).

FRIEND TO THE HURTING

Jesus was a special friend to those who were hurting. He came to bring mercy and alleviate suffering. This was prophesied about him 700 years earlier in Isaiah, "He will not cry aloud or lift up his voice, or make it heard in the street; *a bruised reed he will not break, and a faintly burning wick he will not quench*" (Isa. 42:2-3, emphasis mine).

The imagery of a bruised reed and a faintly burning wick is vivid. It reminds me of someone who is just about to give up. Many times I have felt this way myself. As if a small breeze would do me in.

Jesus came to restore and redeem, but he came gently and with compassion. There are so many stories of Jesus stopping whatever he was doing to minister to someone in need.

One time he was in the middle of a large crowd when a woman with a blood disorder reached out to touch him. When she did she was healed. Jesus didn't scold her for taking advantage of his power, instead he pointed out her faith to those around him (Luke 8:43-48).

Another time he was teaching in a home where the crowd of onlookers was so thick no one could get into the house to be healed. Some men even cut a hole in the roof to let their friend down through the ceiling in order to get to Jesus. He stopped his teaching for a moment and healed the man. He said nothing about the damaged roof (Luke 5:17-39).

One of my favorite examples happened when Jesus was on his way to Jericho in Luke 18. As he walked with the crowd a blind man began to call out to him, "Son of David, have mercy on me!" (v. 38). His shouts got the attention of many in the crowd who told him to be quiet. In their minds, he wasn't worth Jesus's time. But no matter how many times they told him to be quiet he would not stop calling out. He cried out even louder.

When Jesus heard the man the Bible says he 'stopped' and asked the man to be brought to him. That blind man received sight that day because of his faith (v. 43).

Over and over Jesus took the time to help people when and where they needed it most.

YOU'VE GOT A FRIEND

Have you thought of Jesus as a friend like that? Have you thought of him as someone who would stop what they were doing to help you in your greatest time of need? A lot of times I say that Jesus is my friend but deep in my heart and soul, I'm not sure if I believe it or not. This is evident from my prayer life.

When I pray to God I often feel like I might be bothering him—especially if my prayers are about small or insignificant things. I figure, God has so many other important things happening right now, he surely doesn't need to hear about troubles.

But there's a danger in thinking this. It's the idea that God wants to treat us as subjects or underlings, as if he annoyed with us. But Jesus is clear in the scriptures—he sees us as his friends. Though, there's a *tiny* catch.

In John 15 Jesus tells his disciples, "You are my friends *if* you do what I command you" (v. 14). At first glance, this sounds like conditional friendship, as if Jesus can only be our friend if we obey him. But it's more nuanced than that. He was telling his disciples the purpose of his friendship with them is so they will turn around and live the same way he did. He wants them to be a friend to the hurting, the humble, and the hated. His compassion for the lost is a template for the rest of us. And, if we want to consider ourselves *friends* with Jesus we are expected to live in the same way.

Jesus is your friend. It doesn't matter who you are, where you come from, what you've done, or what other people think about you. Now, who can you be that kind of friend to? Who is in your life right now that needs *you* to reach out to them no matter what their past is or how they are looked at by other people? Why not take a moment and think about how you can encourage them? Write a note, send a text, or even call to let them know you're there for them.

> JESUS IS YOUR FRIEND. IT DOESN'T MATTER WHO YOU ARE, WHERE YOU COME FROM, WHAT YOU'VE DONE, OR WHAT OTHER PEOPLE THINK ABOUT YOU.

Jesus is ready to be that kind of friend to you, are you ready to be that kind of friend too?

SIX

BROTHER JESUS

MORE THAN A ONE-DIMENSIONAL SAVIOR

"A man of many companions
may come to ruin, but there
is a friend who sticks
closer than a brother."

—Proverbs 18:24

KIDS TODAY HAVE IT GOOD. Smartphones and tablets make a long drive go by pretty quickly. If you're old enough to remember station wagons then you probably also remember taking those long summer drives on vacation with your family before the advent of handheld devices. Mom and Dad would be luxuriously seated in the front seat while all the kids were packed in the back. It seemed like those trips would take days. Maybe that's because they did. It was too expensive to fly, unless you were a Rockefeller or something. So the majority of us had to play games in the car like, *I Spy*, or *Highway Alphabet*. If we were really lucky we had one of those invisible ink puzzle game books. Remember those?

In truth, my family didn't take too many long trips—at least not like other families. When we did travel, most of the time my brother, sister, and I got along just fine. But every once in awhile we would really have it out for each other. Hitting, screaming, scratching, and gouging for more room in the back seat. You know, basic sibling stuff.

Jesus had brothers and sisters too. Did you know that? It's true. Jesus was not an only child. If you're surprised by this don't worry, most people are.

To be fair, they were his half-siblings. But still, most of the time when we think of Jesus we forget he was raised in a normal family.

In Mark 6:3, Jesus is teaching in the synagogue and someone points out that his own brothers and sisters were in attendance. They say, "Is this not the carpenter, the Son of Mary, and the brother of James, and Joses, and Judas, and Simon? And are not his sisters here with us?..." It's sort of surreal to think about Jesus this way, but it does help us understand his humanity. So much of our life can be shaped by our siblings. Remember, Jesus lived his life free from sin. That's amazing because he had four brothers and at least one sister.

What it must have been like to grow up in the same house with Jesus. I'm sure it was frustrating for his siblings, having to be compared to their older brother. It must have created some sibling rivalry or at least some jealousy.

NO HONOR IN HOUSEHOLD

Living with Jesus must have been tough! Did Jesus always finish his homework first? Did he always remember to make his bed and clean his room? Honestly, I don't even know if young Jewish boys had homework or if they had to make their beds. But if they did, it stands to reason that Jesus was good at it. He was perfect. The Bible says he was tempted in every way but he did not sin (Heb. 4:15).

I can only imagine what kind of sibling rivalry may have developed between Jesus and his brothers and sister. For example, did Mary favor Jesus above her other children?

Put yourself in her sandals for a moment. It would be hard not to treat Jesus differently knowing what you know about your first-born. Besides being conceived miraculously by God himself, the angels told her Jesus would deliver the people from their sins (Matt. 1:21).

How must it have affected Mary when, just days after his birth, her new, little family was stopped in the Temple courtyard by an old man named Simeon. Simeon had spent his life waiting to see the Messiah in person. He took the baby Jesus into his hands and said, "Lord, now you are letting your servant depart in peace...for my eyes have seen your salvation" (Luke 2:28-33). I picture a real *Lion King* moment as Simeon lifts Jesus up over the crowd.

Just after this happened, an old lady named Anna began to speak up. She was a famous prophetess who basically lived at the Temple. She was awaiting the coming Messiah, and when she saw the baby she started telling everyone in the courtyard that he was to be the redemption of all Jerusalem (v. 36-38).

The Bible says Mary and Joseph "marveled" at the things that were said about their son (v. 33). No doubt they realized Jesus was special. How could they not treat him differently than their other children? Whether Mary and Joseph favored Jesus above the other kids we will never know. What we do know is there was some disconnect in the family as Jesus was revealing himself to the world.

Have you heard the phrase "familiarity breeds contempt"? Perhaps it's true. Sometimes Jesus distanced himself from his family. For example, once while he was teaching, someone in the crowd spoke up and told him his mother and his brothers were looking for him. He replied, "Who are my mother and my brothers?...Here are my mother and my brothers! For whoever does the will of God, he is my brother and sister and mother" (Mark 3:31-35).

Obviously, Jesus was trying to make a larger point about the gospel and the need for unity and fellowship for his followers. Still, Jesus's family must have felt a little slighted. After all, how would you feel if your son or older brother denied being related to you? Around this time, Jesus's brothers still did not believe he was the Messiah.

John illustrates this in chapter 7 of his gospel. Jesus had been working near his hometown but his brothers encouraged him to branch out and do some miracles for a larger audience (John 7:3). The yearly Festival of Booths was about to start and they thought it would be a great opportunity for Jesus to gain more attention.

Their motivation is curious though, because according to John, they don't believe in him as Messiah yet. This is astounding. How can you be raised right alongside the Son of God and not believe he is the Son of God?

The brothers clearly needed more proof. Perhaps their faith was still developing. Though they knew he was special, but they weren't ready to acknowledge his lordship. Like many of Jesus's followers, they were hungry to see signs and miracles.

The problem for his brothers, and for the others who were in constant need of a sign, was that Jesus tended to shut down his miraculous nature when that was all the people wanted to see. For example, the first time we are introduced to Jesus's family, the Bible says Jesus didn't perform any miracles simply because the people in his hometown lacked faith (Matt. 13:58).

In reality, family dynamics often cloud our perception. Maybe you've experienced this same thing? It's as if the closer you are to someone, the less likely you are to realize how special they are. This seems to be the case for Jesus too. I'm sure his family loved him dearly, but it wasn't until some time later they fully acknowledged his greatness.

LEARNING FROM THE BEST

In 2011, I preached through the book of James. As an overzealous and relatively new Bible teacher I somehow managed to stretch five chapters of the Bible into 26 weeks of teaching. That is six months of sermons. Sometimes I wonder how my congregation put up with me.

The book of James is all about how important it is to have faith, but also to back that faith up with action. For example, "So also faith by itself, if it does not have works, is dead" (James 2:17). His basic message? If you are going to talk the talk, you better walk the walk!

But here's what blows me away about the book of James. It was written by Jesus's brother. This shows us, that eventually at least one of Jesus's brothers came to believe in him. In fact, James became a key figure in the early spread of Christianity, working with the other disciples and eventually pastoring the church in Jerusalem.

Much later in life James sat down and decided to write a letter to all of the Jewish believers who had been scattered throughout the world. His letter would find its way into the hands of many believers needing to hear how to live out their Christian lives.

Think of it—every idea, every word, every principle in the book of James was written by someone who spent more time with Jesus than practically anyone else on earth.

When James wrote about withstanding trials (James 1:2-4), he could have been remembering something that happened to Jesus when they were just boys. When he wrote about not showing favoritism (chapter 2) he probably recalled so many of the times when Jesus bypassed the rich and wealthy and focused on the poor instead. And when he talked about prayer in chapter five he had to be thinking about Jesus praying. After all, Jesus wrote the book on prayer, literally (Matt. 6:5-15).

> EVERY PRINCIPLE IN THE BOOK OF JAMES WAS WRITTEN BY SOMEONE WHO SPENT MORE TIME WITH JESUS THAN PRACTICALLY ANYONE ELSE ON EARTH.

There are some however, who do not recognize James, the brother of Jesus, as the author of the letter. They say it was a different James. They point out that he doesn't identify himself as the brother of Jesus in the opening verses of the book, instead referring to himself only as a "servant of God and of the Lord Jesus Christ" (James 1:1). I believe this is just humility on James' part. I bet learned it from Jesus, the one he probably shared a bedroom with while they were growing up.

THE CHOICE IS YOURS

For much of my life I didn't have any siblings. It wasn't until my mom married my step-dad when I was seven that I could say I had a brother and a sister. Up until that time I was an only child.

It's kind of great being an only child. All of your parents' attention is lavished on you. You get more presents at Christmas, you always get the top bunk, and there's no one to tell on you when you sneak that extra cookie from the cookie jar.

But, it's kind of lonely too. After all, there's no one to make tent-forts with, tell scary stories to at night, and back you up if you have to fight the mean kid down the street. Yes, that happened to me once!

For all those only-children out there I have spectacular news. You have a brother. You've always had a brother. His name is Jesus.

I agree, at first that sounds unsettling, maybe even a little heretical, but trust me, it's true. The writer of Hebrews talks about it in the second chapter of his letter. I added some clarifying parentheticals so you don't get lost. It says, "For it was fitting that he (God), for whom and by whom all things exist, in bringing many sons to glory (us), should make the founder of their salvation (Jesus) perfect through suffering. For he (Jesus) who sanctifies and those who are sanctified (us) all have one source. That is why he (Jesus) is not ashamed to call them brothers, saying, 'I will tell of your name to my brothers; in the midst of the congregation I will sing your praise'" (Hebrews 2:10-12).

This is amazing isn't it? What the writer is saying is all of us have the same father—Jesus. This is what makes us brothers. He even includes a quote from Psalm 22, which is a prophecy about Jesus, the earlier part of which Jesus quoted when he hung on the cross (Matt. 27:46). The writer of Hebrews is indicating Jesus had anticipated the fact God would bring all of us into one big family. He would bring us into his glory as sanctified sons and daughters through the suffering of his son and our brother, Jesus.

So, how about you? Have you placed your full faith in your brother, Jesus? It took some time for his earthly brothers to do so. They wanted to see more signs and miracles in order to believe. Maybe that describes you too. You might say, "Sure, I'll believe in him. But only if he reveals himself to me."

> YOU HAVE A BROTHER. YOU'VE ALWAYS HAD A BROTHER. HIS NAME IS JESUS.

Thomas, one of Jesus's original 12 disciples was the same way. He had spent three years with Jesus, seeing every miracle. He even heard Jesus predict his own death and resurrection. Still, when the news broke that Jesus was alive he couldn't bring himself to believe. He wanted hard evidence. He said, "Unless I see in his hands the mark of the nails, and place my finger into the mark of the nails, and place my hand into his side, I will never believe" (John 20:25).

That same day Jesus arrived and allowed Thomas to put his hand right into the open wound in his side, proving he was resurrected. Thomas believed, but Jesus took advantage of a teachable moment and said, "Have you believed because you have seen me? Blessed are those who have not seen and yet have believed" (v. 29).

You too have a choice. You can believe based on the evidence you have now. Or, you can hold out for more evidence. Like Thomas, you can declare you need more time and more proof. You might even get it. Or, you can place your faith in Jesus, your brother, right now. The choice is yours!

SEVEN

CREATOR JESUS

MORE THAN A ONE-DIMENSIONAL SAVIOR

"Creativity is intelligence
having fun."

—Unknown

"And God saw everything
that he had made, and behold,
it was very good."

—Genesis 1:31

I LOVE TO MAKE THINGS. I write music, blogs, and books. I bake bread and brew beer. I also like to design and manage web pages. I'm creative because I'm made in God's image and God is, first and foremost, a creator. That's why you like to create things too. Some people think they are not creative, but everyone is creative in some way—even if it's not an artistic one. You might create spreadsheets, or daily meals for your family. You might find creative ways to get your kids to eat their vegetables. However you look at it, as humans we like to make things. It's part of what makes us people.

Jesus was a creator too, but for some reason we don't think of him that way. Most people consider God to be the maker of heaven and earth and picture Jesus as just God's son, seeing his role in the universe as coming much later. But Jesus has always *been,* from the very beginning of time. This is clear in the Bible, but we often overlook it. Unfortunately, this is a huge oversight because Jesus is a critical factor in the creation of the universe. It's not hyperbole to say the universe was created *through* Jesus, and *for* Jesus.

HE WROTE THE CODE

The first clue Jesus was involved in creation is found in Genesis 1:26, "And God said, let us make man in our image." Our image? That's plural! Is there more than one God? Not exactly, but sorta.

The idea that God is more than one individual is known as the *Trinity*. The word trinity is not in the Bible, but the concept is well noted in the New Testament, and suggested in the Old Testament. Trinity means that God is one, yet in his oneness there are three distinct persons. We may struggle with understanding exactly how that all works, but that is why God is God, and we are not.

The gospel of John, starts likes this, "In the beginning was the Word, and the Word was with God, and the Word was God. He was in the beginning with God" (John 1:1-2). John is talking about Jesus.

Jesus was present at the very beginning of time. He was not created later, nor was he just a man who became a god. He was God from the start and was instrumental in the creation of all things.

I have a friend named Ross who has trouble understanding how Jesus could perform miracles. He wonders if Jesus was a really good magician, or perhaps an expert at sleight-of-hand illusions. But to me, it makes perfect sense Jesus can perform miracles because the world was made through Jesus (John 1:3; Col. 1:16; Heb. 1:2).

Remember when the disciples were trying to feed more than 5,000 people? Jesus had asked the disciples to feed them but the best they could do was round up five loaves of bread and two fish. What does Jesus do? He takes their pitiful offering, prays for it, and starts dividing it up. The more he rips, the more bread there is. He keeps ripping off chunks of bread and somehow there is more. He starts dividing the fish, and somehow there is more (Matt. 14:15-21).

My friend Ross thinks this is a miracle, but not because Jesus reproduced mass quantities of fish and bread. He thinks the miracle happened because when the people saw Jesus share what he had, they also shared what they had with each other. So, because there was a spirit of sharing among them, nobody went left hungry.

That's all well and good, but here's what I'm saying. Jesus had a part in hand-crafting the universe. He knows every detail, every molecule, and every atom. He understands the glutenous structure of bread because he *designed* wheat. It's nothing for Jesus to make bread. It's easy for him. Panera has nothing on Jesus.

Think back to Jesus's first miracle. It's one of the best. He was at a wedding when they ran out of wine. His mother pressed him to do something about it. I always wonder, how does she even know that he could do something about it? Probably (and I'm guessing here) because more than a few times while growing up, Jesus might have done a couple miracles here and there around the house—maybe stretched that meatloaf to feed an extra guest or two? Or perhaps turned the water into wine—or grape juice depending on the age of his siblings? She knew he had the ability to do something, so she asked him to help.

At first, Jesus hesitated. He didn't want the publicity and he didn't think it was time to reveal his power. Still, he's a good son, and he eventually agreed to help. His mother told the servants, "Do whatever he tells you" (John 2:5).

The servants filled up 6 huge water jars, each holding between 20 and 30 gallons of water.

After they filled up the jars, he instructed the servants to bring a sample to the head of the servants. The head servant tasted it and declared it to be top-notch wine. The best of the best. John tells us this was a turning point for his disciples. It's when they started to believe in him (John 2:11).

There are those who say this was really just an elaborate trick. Truthfully, I've seen a magician perform a trick like this on *America's Got Talent*. Skeptics say that Jesus had some food coloring or red powder hidden in those jars so that when water was added it turned red. They say the people were already so drunk they didn't even realize they were drinking red water. Seriously, getting people to believe red water is good wine? Now that would be a miracle!

If Jesus was just a normal person, I would have trouble believing it too. If he were just a good man with a good philosophy for life I would think it was a trick. But Jesus was more than that. As part of the Trinity, Jesus shares the privilege of deity with the Father and the Holy Spirit. And as we've said, He was instrumental in the process of creation—including water and grapes! Jesus put the "H" in H_2O. When you think about it like that it's so easy to understand.

It's like one of my favorite movies, *The Matrix*. The main character, Neo, is a guy who learns to see his world in code. In the beginning of the movie, he's subject to all the rules and limitations of his surroundings just like everyone else.

But, by the end of the movie he has learned the secret to the world he's trapped in. It's all just computer program and he has the ability to manipulate the code. Once he realizes he can manipulate the code, he's able to bend or break the rules within his world.

That's the way I see Jesus. He wrote the code; therefore, he can change it, bend it, break it.

In the gospels, Jesus is often one step ahead of people. He knew what the disciples were thinking. He knew what the Pharisees were plotting. How did Jesus know other people's thoughts? Because he is also God, he's an amazing judge of character and knows the hearts of people.

Going back to Genesis 1, it says, "Let us make man in our image" (Gen. 1:26). What does that mean? Does it mean that because we have a nose, God must have a nose? Does it mean because we are bipeds God is also a biped? The obvious answer is no. When it says image it means we share feelings, emotions, intellect, and self-awareness.

> THAT'S THE WAY I SEE JESUS. HE WROTE THE CODE; THEREFORE, HE CAN CHANGE IT, BEND IT, BREAK IT.

The gospel writer Luke tells a story of Jesus's incredible ability to know people. In the story, Jesus had been invited to dine at the home of a Pharisee named Simon. During the meal, a local prostitute crashed the dinner party to anoint Jesus with oil. During the process she made a huge scene because she cannot stop crying and kissing Jesus's feet.

This was embarrassing for Simon. First, the woman was considered unclean by the Pharisees because of her occupation. Second, she was not invited. Watching the scene play out, Simon said to himself, "If this man were a prophet, he would have known who and what sort of woman this is who is touching him" (Luke 7:36-50).

I have often wondered if "said to himself" really means he mumbled it under his breath. Or, does said to himself mean he said it in his mind. When I say things to myself, it's usually in my mind. Nevertheless, Jesus responded with a story. He knew what Simon was thinking, simply because he *knew* Simon. He knew Simon because he *made* Simon. He's the designer of people. He knows how people think.

Have you ever said to a close friend or family member, "I know what you're thinking?" Why do you think you know what someone is thinking? It's because you know the person so well.

I have been married to my wife for 25 years and we dated for four years before that. That means we have been around each other for almost three decades. Believe me, we know what each other is thinking. Sometimes just a quick look, or a sigh, or a smirk is all that we need from each other and we know. I'm sure you're the same way with your spouse, or your kids, or your best friends.

Over and over the gospels tell us that Jesus "knew what they were thinking" (Luke 5:22; Matt. 12:25). But I propose to you this is less of a magic trick and more of an understanding of people. As the maker of humanity, Jesus is tuned into what makes people tick. He understands the feelings of jealousy and pride that we struggle with. He is able to grasp the fact we have issues with self-worth and guilt. He is able to determine what you are thinking at this very moment.

This is troubling to some because the last place they want Jesus to be is in their brain! There's a lot of bad stuff in there. Just remember, Jesus faced every challenge you have faced. Every temptation, every feeling, every hurt. Every single one. The writer of Hebrews reminds us that he was like us in every way so he knows what we are facing (Heb. 4:15). The point is not that we should be ashamed to realize Jesus knows our thoughts, the point is we can come to him with confidence and ask for mercy and grace. Because he designed us, he knows. Because he knows, he understands. And because he lived among us for a time, he feels what we feel.

OUR PURPOSE REVEALED

When I was in 5th grade I played flag football. That's the version of football where no one tackles anyone, but instead everyone wears a couple streamers attached to their belt. If you have the ball and someone pulls off one of your streamers or "flags"—you are down or "tackled."

I didn't get to touch the ball much back then. I played defense. But I was also sort of confused because no one explained to me what I was supposed to be doing. When we lined up on the field, I thought my job was to bump into the guy in front of me, regardless of what was happening with the ball. They said that was called, "blocking." No one told me we were supposed to try and stop the guy with the ball. They just said, "block the guy in front of you." So that's what I did. Meanwhile, their running back could blow right by me without a second thought. I didn't know I was supposed to stop him.

I realize now that it probably looked ridiculous, a bunch of ten-year-olds just bumping into each other. I was confused because I didn't know the overall goal of the team or my role on it.

> IN THE END, EVERY PERSON WILL ADMIT TO HIS GREATNESS AND MAJESTY. EVEN THOSE WHO DIDN'T BELIEVE IN HIM WILL BE FORCED TO ACKNOWLEDGE THE LORDSHIP OF JESUS.

In the same way, many people on earth don't know why they were put here. They simply don't know why they were created. Even if someone might have told them why, most still don't know the end goal.

Because people don't know the goal, they end up just spending a lot of time bumping into each other, unsure of what they're really supposed to be doing in life. This leads a lot of people to believe their end goal is to have a lot of money, fame, or even happiness.

However, in Revelation chapter 4, the end goal is described in brilliant detail. The Apostle John, now well into his 90's, had been exiled to an island called Patmos. While he was there, God gave him a technicolor vision of Heaven and told him to write it down.

He wrote, "and behold, a throne stood in heaven, with one seated on the throne. And he who sat there had the appearance of jasper and carnelian, and around the throne was a rainbow that had the appearance of an emerald. Around the throne were twenty-four thrones, and seated on the thrones were twenty-four elders, clothed in white garments, with golden crowns on their heads. From the throne came flashes of lightning, and rumblings and peals of thunder, and before the throne were burning seven torches of fire, which are the seven spirits of God, and before the throne there was as it were a sea of glass, like crystal" (Rev. 4:1b-6a).

He went on to describe four angelic creatures who also surround the throne. Their only task for eternity is to worship the one who is on the throne. Eventually, John saw an immeasurable number of people surrounding the throne. He says they represent every country in the world, every nationality, and every language. They too, worship Him who is seated on the throne (Rev. 7:9).

When you step back and picture the scene, it's amazing. John is describing exactly what Paul wrote to the church in Philippi when he said, "at the name of Jesus every knee should bow, in heaven and on earth and under the earth, and every tongue confess that Jesus Christ is Lord, to the glory of God the Father" (Phil. 2:10-11).

I'm certain of this: in the end you and I will worship Jesus Christ. In the end, every person will admit to his greatness and majesty. Even those who didn't believe in him will be forced to acknowledge the lordship of Jesus. This makes a lot of sense because more than anything else, you and I were made for worship. It's in our spiritual DNA.

When you hear of isolated tribes, no matter where in the world—none are without some understanding of a higher power or a belief in the spiritual realm. From the very beginning of time, mankind has worshipped the sun, the moon, rain, fertility, and a host of man-made idols. Even the person who says there is no god is worshipping something—perhaps a belief in their own certainty.

In the book of Ecclesiastes, Solomon wrote that God put "eternity into the heart of every man" (Eccl. 3:11). Part of the way we were made involves yearning for something more in our lives. We long for meaning—something greater than ourselves. That longing was placed there on purpose. It's a homing beacon back to God.

In the very beginning of time, Jesus shared a role in creating the universe. God's purpose and plan was to create a place where all things would be in perfect order. He wanted to create a place of perfect communion with the creatures he made. In order to have a true relationship with his created ones, he gave them free-will. He created us with the ability to choose or reject him. Because we soon rejected him, God sent his son, Jesus to make all things right. This was done through Jesus's sacrifice of death, made for all people.

As a result, God placed Jesus Christ at the center of this corrected universe, so that eventually, all creatures would worship him. That was what John saw in his vision on Patmos.

Allow me to melt your mind for a moment. The vision that was described in such striking and colorful detail by John is waiting for you. You will see it one day. You'll see it exactly how he described it—the thunder, lightning, the 24 elders, the four angels, the throngs of people worshipping. You'll see it whether you want to or not. Because when that day comes you'll know without a shadow of a doubt who Jesus is and what he did for you.

I'm looking forward to that day. I hope you are too. As a matter of fact, we don't have to wait to start worshipping like that. Because this worship is happening right now in Heaven, *and* on earth. It happens every time people gather in the name of Christ. It happens every time someone decides to follow Christ. It happens every sunrise and sunset. If you see Jesus for who he really is, then it can be happening for you every moment of every day.

Jesus Christ, the creator, designed you with a purpose. Your purpose is more than just making money, earning a good reputation among your peers, or even the pursuit of happiness. Your purpose is to have a meaningful relationship with God and to worship him in this life—and the next.

EiGHT
MESSIAH JESUS

MORE THAN A ONE-DIMENSIONAL SAVIOR

"Behold, the days are coming, declares the Lord, when I will raise up for David a righteous Branch, and he shall reign as king and deal wisely, and shall execute justice and righteousness in the land."

—Jeremiah 23:5

EVERY YEAR FOR MY KIDS' birthdays we give them the choice of where to eat out. They can pick any restaurant, within reason, to celebrate their birthday. When my son was younger he always chose The Golden Corral. If you have never been there, The Golden Corral is a giant buffet that features every kind of food you can imagine. Want a steak? No problem. How about Chinese? Yep, they have that too. And dessert? Don't get me started on dessert. It was hard to convince my kids to at least eat something reasonably healthy before taking advantage of the dessert bar.

There was a town in the first century similar to this restaurant. It was called Caesarea Philippi. The town was a buffet of different religions. This town was strategically located on a trade route north of Galilee. Because of this location, it was a melting pot of various beliefs and spiritual ideologies.

In Matthew 16, Jesus was with his disciples in Caesarea Philippi when he asked them an important question. He asked, "Who do people say that the Son of man is?" (v. 13). Against the backdrop of these many beliefs and religions, it was kind of a trick question. The disciples racked their brains for the right answer. Was Jesus talking about himself in third person again (he liked to do that), or was he talking about someone else?

Somewhat stumped, the disciples throw a couple of obvious answers back, "John the Baptist, Elijah, Jeremiah, one of the prophets?" (v. 14). Each answer was really a question. Then Jesus changed it up and asked them straight out: "But who do *you* say that I am?" (v. 15). At this point Simon Peter stepped forward. I imagine him looking Jesus right in the eye as he says, "You are the Christ, the Son of the living God" (v. 16). He nailed it! 10 points and a star for Peter.

Why is it so important to really know who Jesus is? Why spend so much time trying to understand his personality, his motives, and his actions? It's simple. If we don't truly know who Jesus is, it is possible for us to focus on an inaccurate version of Jesus, or to miss him completely.

In Acts 13, about 10 years after the death of Jesus, Paul and his friend Barnabas went to the Greco-Roman city of Antioch. On the Sabbath they entered the synagogue and were given the chance to teach. Paul preached an amazing sermon to the Jews in attendance. He told them God had been hinting at the coming Messiah for centuries. He reminded them about Moses, the judges, Samuel, and David—all of whom alluded to the coming of King Jesus. In verse 27 he said, "because they did not recognize him nor understand the utterances of the prophets, which are read every Sabbath, fulfilled them by condemning him."

Paul's message is blunt. He told them the Messiah had been right in front of them the whole time. It was in the writings, which they studied every Sabbath in the synagogue. Even though it was preached to them every week, they still missed it! Even worse, in rejecting Jesus and then condemning him to death, they actually fulfilled the very prophecies in the scriptures that were put in place to help them see Jesus.

We are in danger of this today too. If we don't know who Jesus is, or if we have the wrong idea about his character, his attitude, orhis humanity then it's possible we too will miss him. Think of it, countless people sit in church every Sunday, and in many of those churches they are only taught about the serious Jesus, the weakling Jesus, the wimpy Jesus. Then, when the real Jesus is presented to them, the one that is truthful, playful, consequential, and strong— they miss him.

I think this is why so many young people leave their faith. According to USA Today, 70% of young Christians leave the church after high school.[14] It's because they haven't been introduced to the life-changing, relatable, holy Messiah. The Messiah that demands something from them. The Messiah who calls them to a greater commitment.

If young people are brought up in a church that allows them to treat Jesus the same way you would act at a buffet— *I'll take a little of his grace and love, but this long-term, life commitment? I can't stomach that*—then we should not be surprised when people leave the church. See, it's easy to leave a church, but it's hard to leave Jesus.

> SEE, IT'S EASY TO LEAVE A CHURCH, BUT IT'S HARD TO LEAVE JESUS.

---

14 Cathy Lynn Grossman, "Young Adults Aren't Sticking with Church: 70% of surveyed Protestants Stopped Attending by Age 23," *USA Today*, https://usatoday30.usatoday.com/printedition/life/20070807/d_churchdropout07.art.htm (accessed November 12, 2017).

GO AHEAD, COPYCAT

When John wrote his first epistle, 1 John, close to the end of the first century, it was to make sure people were following the right Messiah. He tells his readers others will know whether they are truly Christians by how they act: "whoever says he abides in him ought to walk in the same way in which he walked" (1 John 2:6).

It's important to make sure we follow the right version of Jesus, the biblical version, because this is how we will copy Jesus in our own lives. If the Jesus you follow is weak, then you'll be weak. If the Jesus you follow is unapproachable, you too will be unapproachable.

Instead, realize and remember the real Jesus was not only approachable, but affable and funny. If you follow that Jesus, then this is how you can be too, approachable and not afraid of humor.

Remember the kind of people who were naturally drawn to Jesus: sinners and children. I know it's a strange combination, but it says a lot about his character. Besides being friendly, Jesus was also nonjudgmental. This characteristic is what allowed prostitutes, thieves, and other sinners to become close to Jesus.

Jesus was also tough and he didn't suffer religious fools. If you walk like Jesus then you'll be able to stand up to religious zealots, the kind of people who love rules and regulations, but are far from God. You'll also be able to be friends with people who are not religious and those who have given up on the religious system. Just as Jesus was welcomed into these circles, you will be too.

There are so many more characteristics we haven't talked about in this book. If you copy the real Jesus, you will be able to imitate these too. For example, Jesus was humble and forgiving. He was also emotional and allowed himself to cry in front of his friends. Don't mistake this for weakness. Showing true emotion is a mark of strong character and being self-assured.

All of these characteristics and more are listed in the New Testament Gospels: Matthew, Mark, Luke, and John. Don't take my word for it—read it for yourself. If you pay careful attention you will see traits of Jesus that you might have overlooked.

That's why it's so important we get this right. We represent Jesus to the world. Rather than show everybody a fake, one-dimensional Jesus, let's show them the real, fully human, deeply loving, three-dimensional Jesus.

DON'T MISS HIM

Recently, I bought lunch at a local sub shop. When I received my change, I put the money in my pocket and thought nothing of it. However, later on I noticed one of the bills given to me with my change was a little off. It just didn't look right, and the paper felt different. It turns out I received a counterfeit $5 bill with my change.

Counterfeiting is a big problem in the United States. The danger of having fake currency in our economy is the effect it has on real currency; it devalues it. Counterfeiting also causes inflation. Plus, the more fake money in the system, the less real money is trusted.

The same is true when it comes to counterfeiting Jesus. When millions of Christians are copying the wrong version of Jesus then the real Jesus is devalued and not trusted. The worst-case scenario is the world might miss him too. This really scares me. If you're a believer in Jesus it should scare you too. The last thing we want to do is portray the wrong Jesus to people in need of a real savior.

There's an amazing account of this happening in the book of Acts, chapter 19. God had been doing miracles through Paul. In the same area, there were some brothers known as "the seven sons of Sceva" (Acts 19:14).[15] As they witnessed these miracles they decided to try to perform a few of their own. The seven sons of Sceva found a man who was possessed with an evil spirit and tried to cast the demon out. However, the evil spirit answered them by asking, "Jesus I know, and Paul I recognize, but who are you?" (v. 15). Who knew demons had a sense of humor? It's the first century equivalent of 'who dis?'

Have you heard the phrase, "You're the only Bible some people will ever read?" Whether that's true I'm not sure. What I do know is, you're the only Jesus some people will ever see. As we talked about before, 1 John 2:6 says,

---

15   Sceva was a Jewish high priest.

"Whoever says he abides in him ought to walk in the same way in which he walked." If you're a Christian then you are a walking, talking copy of Jesus and so am I. When we become more like Jesus, the world around us will see our actions and say, "yeah, I want to know that Jesus more." Unfortunately, I've spoken to many who have said the opposite. They tell me, "No, I've seen how Christians treat each other. I've read your web sites and heard your political agendas. I've even visited your churches and watched your actions closely. If that's Jesus, then, no thank you. I can live without that."

Sadly, they are right. In so many cases what they are seeing is not the real Jesus at all, but a fake one. A poor counterfeit Jesus. They see versions of Jesus that don't forgive and hold grudges. Or they've seen a carefully crafted Jesus—tailored to fit our agendas and purposes. They've been watching a tamed, softened, polished Jesus that seems acceptable to all, but consequential to no one. Truth be told, we can all live without that Jesus.

But the real Jesus? No, you can't live without him. The famous 19th century preacher Charles Spurgeon may have said it best: "I would propose...that the subject of the ministry of this house, as long as this platform shall stand, and as long as this house shall be frequented by worshipers, shall be the person of Jesus Christ."[16] Spurgeon was talking about the real Jesus.

---

16   Drummond, Lewis A. *Spurgeon: Prince of Preachers.* (Grand Rapids: Kregel, 1992).

So where do you stand? What version of Jesus have you been copying? By now, I hope you are beginning to appreciate a more accurate version of Jesus. The Jesus who can't be ignored, yet doesn't force you into following him. This is a Jesus both men and women can copy. He's full of integrity and grit, but is also humble and can share a laugh with friends.

If you haven't been copying this Jesus I invite you to follow him today. If you do, you will be able to share an accurate picture of Jesus with the world, and believe me, the world is in dire need of that picture. Be funny, be tough. When you need to, be rebellious too. Follow the example of Jesus Christ, and be a good friend, and good brother or sister to all. When the Apostle Paul encouraged his readers to be imitators and "walk in love, as Christ loved us" (Eph. 5:2a), his hope was that the Ephesians would forgive and sacrifice like Jesus. He wanted them to be like Jesus.

And that is my hope for you too.

SMALL GROUP &
PERSONAL BIBLE STUDY

WHILE MOST OF THE OTHER kids in my high school took driver's ed after school, somehow I missed the cutoff to sign up. My mother then signed me up for drivers training at the Sears Driving School (yes, *that* Sears) where "good drivers are safe drivers." It was humiliating for me to miss the deadline and have to take drivers training at Sears, of all place, but my embarrassment didn't stop there. What happened during one of the driving tests was eye opening—literally.

I was driving the test car down the road along with a couple other students and the instructor. When the instructor told me to exit the road at the sign marked "77," I said okay and then drove right past the next off-ramp. He asked me why I didn't exit and I told him I thought the sign said, "11" not "77." I was fitted for glasses that same week.

Up until that time I hadn't realized my vision was going bad. It had been happening so slowly I didn't notice everything was a little fuzzy. When I put my glasses on for the first time I felt like I was on an alien planet. Everything was so colorful, so vivid, so detailed.

When I started creating this material, originally as a teaching series for my congregation, and eventually as a book, my only goal was to help people get a more vivid and detailed picture of Christ. While in the process of researching more about Jesus I ended up upgrading my own spiritual prescription for Jesus as well. That's the amazing thing about the Bible and Jesus. No matter how much you know, there's always something new to discover, or some surprising insight you may have missed before.

So, whether you're new to Jesus Christ or you've been a follower of his for decades. I invite you take your understanding of the Savior to the next level. I have created this companion study guide as a way for you to dig into the scriptures for yourself. Use this guide for your personal quiet time, with a Bible study partner, or share it in a small group setting.

I'm hoping it will allow you a 20x20 view into the life and character of our amazing Lord, Jesus Christ. To him be the glory forever, Amen!

Funny Jesus

Key Verse

"These things I have spoken to you, that my joy may be in you, and that your joy may be full."

—John 15:11

Key Scripture

John 15:1-11

THIS YEAR I STARTED COMPILING a list of my favorite jokes. I'm not above starting a sermon with a joke. It sets the mood for the congregation and usually helps build some momentum for the sermon.

There's just something about laughter that brings joy. While we rarely picture Jesus laughing, I am confident he had a fully developed sense of humor. According to the gospel writer John, Jesus possessed a great sense of joy (John 15:11), and since everything about Jesus is ultimately perfect, then we know his joy was perfect as well.

Of course, Joy isn't just about laughter, happiness, or having a sense of humor. Joy is bigger than that. Joy is the ability to maintain your sense of humor and happiness despite your circumstances. There's not always laughter in joy, but there's always joy in true laughter.

SEE FOR YOURSELF

Read John 15:1-11.

What is Jesus asking his disciples to do in this passage? (v. 4)

What two guarantees does Jesus make if we can remain (abide) in him? (v. 7 & 11)

THINK ABOUT IT

List 3 people you enjoy hanging out with (other than Jesus).

  1.
  2.
  3.

Put a checkmark next to the people that have a good sense of humor. Is that part of what attracts you to their friendship?

Do they also have a good sense of humor, and do they have sense of joy?

Rate your own sense of humor on a scale from 1 to 10.

TALK ABOUT IT

Discuss the value of copying Jesus's playful sense of humor and easygoing nature. Is it a help to the cause of the gospel, or a hindrance? Why?

Tough Jesus

Key Verse

"And he told those who sold the pigeons, 'Take these things away; do not make my Father's house a house of trade.'"

—John 2:16

Key Scripture

John 2:13-22

A FEW YEARS BACK MY wife and I drove to Ponte Vedra Beach, Florida to watch the Players Championship Golf Tournament. We're big golf fans and try to attend local tournaments whenever we can.

That day we had purchased snacks and drinks at the local market, and slid them into our pockets and bag knowing the high cost of purchasing concessions within the park. Of course, on the way into the event, security was stopping everyone and asking them to empty their pockets. Spectators were being forced to leave their waters, sodas, and snacks outside the park before entry. They were on to us. I had to dump my whole stash of food in the garbage before entering the event. A few hours later we were parched and hungry and forced to pay a whopping $24 for two sodas, a bag of chips, and one pitiful hot dog. What a gouging!

When Jesus cleared the temple of the money changers, it was because they were being gouged as well. In the first century, all of Judea was under Roman control and most people used Roman currency to buy and sell goods. However, the Jewish temple forbade the use of Roman currency because it contained a graven image (Exod. 20:4). Because of this, a group of merchants known as "money changers" were able to take advantage of thousands of temple goers. They would exchange the Roman currency for a shekel, or a Jewish coin, one that was fit for donation in the temple. Of course, this exchange included a surcharge. Since there was nowhere else to exchange money, innocent worshippers were forced to pay the surcharge.

Those who sold animals were also in on the scam. Because The Law stated that no animals with a defect could be offered (Deut. 17:1), priests would reject many of the animals that were brought by the worshippers for sacrifice. However, an approved animal sacrifice could be purchased inside the temple for a high price. No doubt the priests received their cut from the sale too.

SEE FOR YOURSELF

Read John 2:13-22.

What community-wide event was taking place when Jesus arrived at the temple? (v. 13)

Why do you think Jesus was angry with the money changers and people selling animals?

THINK ABOUT IT

In your opinion, is it OK for churches to sell things on Sundays? For example, coffee, mugs, books, or tickets to upcoming events?

Why or why not?

TALK ABOUT IT

Have you ever been to a church where you felt pressured to give more money than you can afford?

How does this new picture of Jesus affect your view of him? Does it draw you closer, or further from him?

Rebel Jesus

Key Verse

Then he said to them, "Therefore render to Caesar the things that are Caesar's, and to God the things that are God's."

—Matthew 22:21

Key Scripture

Matthew 22:15-22

THE FIRST TIME I ASSOCIATED anything positive with the word "rebel" was when I was about 7 years old. After some debate about whether it was an appropriate movie for me to attend, my parents took me to see *Star Wars: A New Hope.*

In the movie, the Empire was bearing down on the galaxy, imposing draconian rules on peaceful planets. At the head of it all was the dreaded Darth Vader. However, a small *Rebel Alliance* was forming to stand against the imposed rule of the Empire—hoping to thwart their progress and save the universe. The Rebel Alliance were the good guys, lead by Princess Leia, Luke Skywalker, and Han Solo.

Sometimes, rebellion is a good thing—as long as you're rebelling against the right people for the right reasons. Jesus was one such rebel. Though he never broke any of the Old Testament commandments and upheld Old Testament Law perfectly, he was willing to stand against an "empire" abusing its power for profit and gain.

In Matthew 22:15-22, Jesus tangles with agents of this so-called empire, the Pharisees. The Romans had conquered the Judean countryside, offering the citizens of Jerusalem religious freedom and peace, though at a high cost. The Jews were free to worship as long as they paid their taxes and didn't cause too much trouble for the local Roman authorities. The Pharisees helped to broker this peace by placating the local foreign rulers while encouraging their Jewish countrymen to remain constrained.

The Pharisees thought they could trick Jesus into denying the Roman government taxes, thereby making Jesus susceptible to the legal repercussions of tax evasion. As on other occasions, he was able to outwit them again.

SEE FOR YOURSELF

Read Matthew 22:15-22.

What was the goal of the Pharisees and the Herodians in asking Jesus about tax? (v. 15)

THINK ABOUT IT

In verse 18, Jesus calls them "hypocrites." Can you think of any reason he would label them this way? Hint: Read Exodus 20:4.

TALK ABOUT IT

Has there ever been a time you were rebellious, but it was for the *right* reason?

Teacher Jesus

Key Verse

"Other seeds fell on good soil and produced grain, some a hundredfold, some sixty, some thirty. He who has ears, let him hear."

—Matthew 13:8-9

Key Scripture

Matthew 13:1-9

IN CHAPTER 7, I MENTIONED I like to brew beer. You may be okay with that, or you might be wondering how a pastor could justify such an activity. In my mind, if Jesus created wine then it's got to be acceptable for a pastor to brew beer!

One of the reasons I enjoy this hobby so much is that it represents a blend of cooking, science, and art. As a brewer, I create a recipe and decide how much of each ingredient is used to make the beer. Truth be told, there's not much that goes into beer: water, barley, yeast, and hops, that's it. It's the hops that give the beer it's bite.

When I first started making beer, I wanted to grow the hops myself. Hops are actually a flower that grows on a vine. You pick the hop flowers before they bloom, dry them, and add them to the beer during the brewing process and sometimes during fermentation too. There was only one problem with me trying to grow hops—I live in Central Florida. The sun and the soil are all wrong to grow this type of plant. The soil in Florida is sandy and very low in nutrients. I tried all kinds of different ways to grow hops: in the ground, in pots, buckets, and even through hydroponics. No matter what I tried it just didn't work. Each time the vines would start by growing and showing promise, but eventually the hot, Florida sun would dry them up and they would die.

Jesus told a similar story in the Bible, albeit not about hops, but specifically about seeds. In the story, he talked about a man who was planting some seeds by scattering them along the ground as he walked. As he went, the seeds fell onto different kinds of ground. Some fell onto a hard path, some fell onto thorny ground, some were eaten up by birds, and some fell onto good soil. I'm sure you can guess what happened—the only seeds that actually grew into strong, healthy plants were the ones that fell onto good soil.

SEE FOR YOURSELF

Read Matthew 13:1-9 and then answer the following questions.

List the different types of soil Jesus talks about.

1.
2.
3.
4.

What was the result of the seed that fell on good soil?

THINK ABOUT IT

Many people believe that the parable of the sower is simply an allegorical way to represent the gospel being preached to non-believers. Is it possible the parable has larger implications than just evangelism? Why or why not?

Jesus explains each type of soil in Matthew 13:18-23. Which type of soil represents your heart most closely right now?

TALK ABOUT IT

What are some things you can do to help maintain healthy soil in your life?

Friend Jesus

Key Verse

"By this we know love, that he laid down his life for us, and we ought to lay down our lives for the brothers."

—1 John 3:16

Key Scripture

John 15:12-15

LT. JOHN ROBERT FOX WAS killed in action on December 26, 1944 in a tiny village in Italy. The fact that he was killed is not unique, however, the events leading up to his death are what make men legendary.

Lt. Fox was part of the "Buffalo Soldiers," an African American division of men that fought on the Italian front during World War II. His regiment was in danger of being overrun by German soldiers when the order to evacuate came from division leadership. However, Fox volunteered to stay behind with a small group of Italian infantry men so he could monitor enemy movement and feed coordinates to a nearby artillery squadron.

Whiile Fox watched the German soldiers swarm the street from the second story of a nearby building, he prepared to radio their position to the artillery squadron. Knowing the only way to defeat the enemy was to sacrifice himself, Fox called in his own position. The blast killed more than 100 enemy soldiers, and Lt. John Fox as well.

For his bravery and sacrifice, Lt. Fox was posthumously awarded the highest honor the military can give, the Medal of Honor.

Jesus willingly gave his life too, not just for his friends, but for his enemies too.

SEE FOR YOURSELF

Read John 15:12-15.

What is the command that Jesus gives his followers? (v. 12)

What is the truest test of love, according to Jesus? (v. 13)

THINK ABOUT IT

According to Jesus, the disciples are not just servants of Jesus, but friends. What are some differences between the two?

While we may never have the chance to give our very lives for our friends, what are some things we can do to show great love for others?

TALK IT THROUGH

Besides Jesus, who is the best example of a friend you can think of?

Who can you make sacrifices for in order to show them your love and friendship?

Brother Jesus

Key Verse

"For if anyone is a hearer of the word and not a doer, he is like a man who looks intently at his natural face in a mirror. For he looks at himself and goes away and at once forgets what he was like."

—James 2:23-24

Key Scripture

James 2:19-27

TAKE A MOMENT AND THINK about all the mirrors you have in your home. Now, count them. Don't forget the mirrors in the bathroom, bedroom, and even the closets. Plus, don't forget any handheld mirrors you might have tucked away in a drawer somewhere. I have more than 15 mirrors in my house. How many do you have?

If you're like me, you're probably surprised by how many mirrors you own. Mirrors have a very basic purpose—to reflect your own image back to you. The better the mirror, the better you can see yourself.

When James, the brother of Jesus, wrote his letter he talked about using Scripture the way we use mirrors. He said, "For if anyone is a hearer of the word and not a doer, he is like a man who looks intently at his natural face in a mirror. For he looks at himself and goes away and at once forgets what he was like" (James 2:23-24).

I can't help but think how James had his own brother to use as perfect example of someone who read the word and then followed it. For James and Jesus, the Word was the Old Testament. For us today, it's both the Old and New Testament.

SEE FOR YOURSELF

Read James 2:19-27.

What is the overall negative characteristic James hopes his readers will be able to avoid?

What part of the body does James think needs to be controlled more than the others?

THINK ABOUT IT

James says it's important to listen. Give yourself a grade, A,B,C,D, or F. What kind of listener are you?

What could you do to become a better listener?

TALK ABOUT IT

In James 2:26, it says it's important to control what we say. How does speaking negatively affect the people around you?

Creator Jesus

Key Verse

"For by him all things were created, in heaven and on earth, visible and invisible, whether thrones or dominions or rulers or authorities—all things were created through him and for him."

—Colossians 1:16

Key Scripture

Colossians 1:15-20

A POPULAR SERMON ILLUSTRATION TELLS the story of a young boy who built a toy boat. He spent time carefully crafting the boat, sanding it, painting it, and eventually carving his initials on the hull. It was beautiful. When he took the boat to a nearby lake to test it out he lost the boat. He had made it so well the wind took the little vessel far from the shore and out of sight. It was gone.

Weeks later he was walking past a toy shop and noticed his boat in the window of the store. He was thrilled! He entered the shop to tell the shopkeeper the boat belonged to him, but even after showing the man his own initials, carved into the boat, the shopkeeper would not give it back to him. The shopkeeper said the boat was for sale, and if the boy wanted it back he had to buy it.

And so he did, spending every last penny he had.

During the first century, not everyone was convinced Jesus Christ was God, nor that he had taken part in creating the universe. Some considered Jesus indeed to be special, but failed to fully recognize his equality with God. Others considered him a Messiah for the Jews, without realizing his role as creator and savior of all mankind, Jew and Gentile alike.

Paul's goal in writing the letter to the Colossians was to assure the early believers that Jesus is Savior, Lord, Messiah, and Creator. By pointing out that all things were created through him (Col 1:16), Paul confirms the authority of Jesus over creation.

SEE FOR YOURSELF

Read Colossians 1:15-20.

Jesus created all things in _____ and _____ (v. 16)

He created things both VISIBLE and _____ (v. 16).

All things were created _____ him and _____ him (v. 16).

THINK ABOUT IT

What does it mean to know that Jesus created all things?

How does that change the way we should respond to him as Lord?

TALK ABOUT IT

List 5 things you enjoy creating or making:

1.
2.
3.
4.
5.

How does knowing you are made in the image of a creator affect your creativity? Or, does it?

Messiah Jesus

Key Verse

"For those who live in Jerusalem and their rulers, because they did not recognize him nor understand the utterances of the prophets, which are read every Sabbath, fulfilled them by condemning him."

—Acts 13:27

Key Scripture

Acts 13:16-41

IF YOU TRAVEL TO A small village just outside of Brasília, Brazil, you will find a man named Álvaro Theiss, though he doesn't go by that name anymore. He calls himself "INRI Cristo." INRI Cristo believes he is Jesus Christ reincarnated. He lives in a compound he has dubbed "New Jerusalem" with his 12 disciples—three men and nine women.

He believes he is Jesus Christ because he heard a voice in his head tell him so. Not everyone agrees, however, because if you go to his Facebook page his rating is just 3.3 stars. Some people think he's the real deal, but naturally most think he is insane.

In the first century, there were many people who also professed to be the messiah. Jesus was not the first or last to make that claim. While John the Baptist never said he was the Christ, many Jews considered him to be the messiah. So much so that when John penned his first gospel he had to remind people that John (not John the Baptist, John the disciple) was not "the light," he was only the one sent to bear witness to the true light (John 1:6-8).

While many were on the lookout for a messiah, few really understood what they were to be looking for. Various prophecies over the years had been misunderstood and people were expecting a mighty military warrior and a man who would bring an end to Roman oppression.

SEE FOR YOURSELF

Read Acts 13:16-41.

What important Jewish figure does Paul trace the lineage of Jesus to? (v. 22)

Who does Paul quote in referring to Jesus? (v. 33; 34)

THINK ABOUT IT

Why is it important for Paul to include the Jewish history in his speech?

List the key people who are mentioned:

TALK ABOUT IT

Why did the Jews misunderstand the prophecies regarding Jesus?

How is it possible for modern believers to misunderstand the person of Jesus as well?